How to Play Cricket Australian Style

Best Wishes Haw,
on your 21ˢᵗ
Joe & Maggie.

INSIDE COVER:-
SIMON BARRY
BOWLING AT
GRANGE NETS.

How to Play Cricket Australian Style

edited by

John Dunn

SOUVENIR PRESS

Contents

Frontispiece : Terry Jenner makes a fine study as he practises at the nets.

Acknowledgements

Rothmans National Sports Foundation for kindly supplying their library of instructional illustrations which portray so well the basic principles of the game
Richie Benaud, Jim Main, Rod Nicholson, Austin Robertson, Alan Shiell and Phil Tresidder for their editorial assistance
Lester Howard for the magic-eye strips
The Herald and Weekly Times Ltd., Melbourne, for the principal photographs and Don Richards for his help in their selection
The Advertiser, Adelaide ; the West Australian, Perth ; the Courier-Mail and the Telegraph, Brisbane ; the Daily Express, London ; Reuters Ltd., London and Central Press, London, for the other pictures
Patrick Eager, Surrey, England, for the colour covers
The Marylebone Cricket Club, London, for the laws of the game.

First British Edition
Published 1975
by Souvenir Press Ltd.

Printed in Hong Kong
SBN 285622005

History

The Third Reich's eagle of war clouded the world from 1939 to 1945 and during these six years cricket mostly was confined to barracks. Wherever British or Australian troops gathered there were cricket matches, and when peace finally came an Australian Services team was formed in England. The team boasted two brilliant players in Lindsay Hassett and Keith Miller. These two players, together with such fine cricketers as Sid Barnes, Don Tallon and Ray Lindwall who were back in Australia, became the nucleus of the great Australian teams of the immediate post-war era. And, of course, the team had as its cornerstone the immortal Don Bradman.

The ink was no sooner dry on peace treaties than Australia was planning for the 1946–47 tour by England. The English arrived with high hopes, but sailed for home with their hopes dashed. The Australians were due to tour England in 1948 and prepared themselves in the summer of 1947–48 against India, led by Armanath. It was India's first tour of Australia, and it turned out to be an unhappy one for them. Australia won four of the five Tests (the other was washed out) and Bradman averaged 178!

Enormous crowds welcomed the return of the Australians to England in 1948. More than 159,000 people saw the Leeds Test and a record crowd of 133,000 watched the Manchester clash. Bradman's superb batting was the spark that rekindled the old Ashes fire. He scored 11 centuries on the tour and notched 2,428 runs

at an average of 89. Not bad for a man approaching his fortieth birthday! But Bradman did not steal the spotlight entirely. The Australians had brilliant openers in Morris and Barnes, and young Neil Harvey scored a century in his maiden Test. The English also had to contend with Miller and Lindwall, plus an eager support fast bowler in Bill Johnston.

The English team was not without its stars. The batting line-up included Len Hutton, Denis Compton and Bill Edrich while there was a good fast bowler in Alec Bedser and a young off-spinner who later became the scourge of Australia. His name? Jim Laker. But Australia took this series four-nil.

Bradman left the Test arena after the 1948 tour and it looked as though England would at last be able to match the Australians. So England tried again in 1950–51 after taking a surprise drubbing against the West Indies in England in 1950. But the Australians, under Lindsay Hassett's leadership, were still in a class of their own although England salvaged some pride by winning the Fifth Test at Melbourne. It was England's first Test Victory over Australia since the war.

It was then the West Indies' turn to try to topple Australia. Goddard led a tremendously enthusiastic team to Australia in 1951, but the West Indies failed. Three years later the return rubber was held in the West Indies where the West Indians were humbled by the Australian's run feast; Neil Harvey averaged 108. The series gave little hint of the magnificent cricket to

1

come in the next Australia-West Indies series.

In between the West Indies diversions Australia lost the Ashes in England in 1953. Four of the five Tests were drawn, with England winning the other Test and sparking tremendous national fervour across the Home Counties. The Fifth Test at The Oval was the deciding match and Tony Lock and Jim Laker were England's hereos. England brought in youngsters Peter May and Fred Trueman for this match and won by eight wickets.

Ian Johnson took over as Australian captain for the 1954–55 series, but England, mainly through Frank Tyson and Brian Statham's pace bowling, took the series three-one. England also won the 1956 series in England under Peter May's captaincy.

This was the year of 'Laker's match', when the great off-spinner Jim Laker took a record 19 wickets for 90 between periods of lashing rain at Manchester. Only Colin McDonald, who batted five and a half hours for 89 runs in the second innings, and to a lesser extent Richie Benaud, offered any resistance. Tony Lock took the only other Australian wicket in the match.

Australia visited India for the first time in 1956 and gave the locals a hard time, winning two Tests and drawing the other. Australia played a five-Test series in India in 1959–60, winning two, drawing two and losing the Second Test at Kanpur by 119 runs. Australia also won a series three-nil in South Africa in 1957–58, under the captaincy of young Ian Craig.

England toured Australia again in 1958–59 and waiting for them was Australian captain, wily Richie Benaud, who was to become one of

Cricket was a leisurely affair in the old days. There was even time for a chat at square leg.

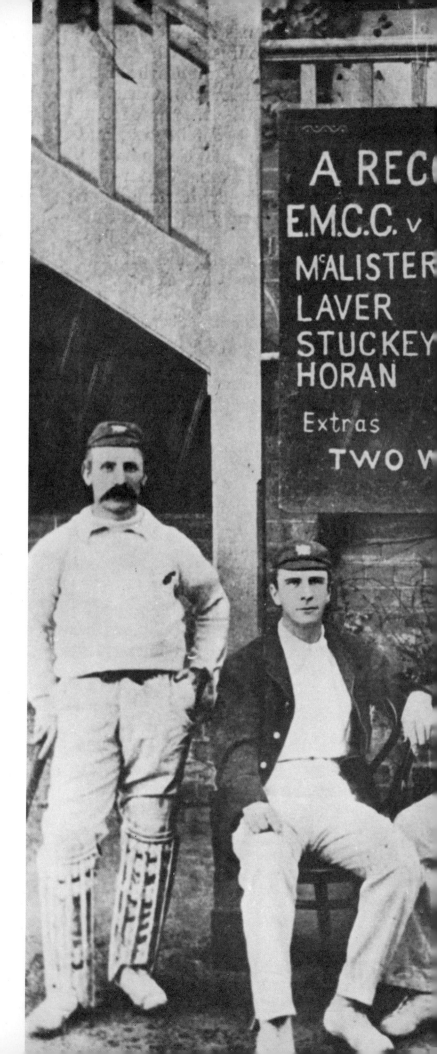

East Melbourne players, (from left) J. H. Stuckey, P. A. McAlister, F. Laver and J. Horan—who in 1903, against Fitzroy, set a world record 744 for two wickets.

Australia's greatest-ever captains. Peter May led the England team of 16, which was without Jim Laker. Ted Dexter was flown out as an extra for a badly injured team, but by this time the series was lost and the ashes back in Australia. Australia's heroes included Benaud, speedsters Alan Davidson and Ian Meckiff, and batsmen Colin McDonald, Jim Burke and Norm O'Neill. Australia won the series four-nil, the Third Test in Sydney being drawn.

Benaud's reign as Australia's cricket captain was a healthy period for Australian cricket. The Australians were almost unbeatable and held off England's challenges for the Ashes in 1961 and 1962–63. Peter May led the England team in England in 1961, and Ted Dexter took over for the 1962–63 touring party which tied the series one-one.

The 1962–63 Ashes series was almost an anti-climax as the 1960–61 West Indies tour of Australia had seen some of the finest cricket ever played. Under Frank Worrell's captaincy the West Indies tied the First Test at Brisbane, the only tied Test match. It certainly guaranteed box-office for the rest of the tour.

Each team won a Test up to the Fifth Test, making this match, at Melbourne, vital. Australia won by two wickets as Melbourne fans were treated to a 1,227 run spectacular. The calypso cricket shot the game into public consciousness and the West Indies team was given a farewell reception in Melbourne as thanks for its entertaining cricket. Maroon and white streamers (the West Indies colours) fluttered down on the visitors as they drove through the streets of Melbourne to a deafening reception. There was no doubt that this was the greatest series yet played, and players like Wes Hall, Charlie Griffith, Seymour Nurse and Joe Valentine will long be remembered with affection in Australia.

England-Australia series remained as dry as ever, despite Australia's slight superiority during the sixties. Australia toured England in 1964 and one Test win under Bobby Simpson was enough to clinch the rubber, as the other four Tests were drawn. In 1965–66 in Australia

each team won a Test, with the other three drawn. Australia again were led by Simpson, while Mike Smith was the English captain. This pattern was repeated in England in 1968 under captains Bill Lawry and Colin Cowdrey.

However, England was not to be denied the Ashes forever, and under the astute Ray Illingsworth the team waged a dour war against Bill Lawry's home team in 1970. It was a long, bitter summer, with seven Tests being played, although one Melbourne Test was washed out after the toss. England, with John Snow hurling down his rockets at timid Australian bats, blasted their way to a two-nil win in the series, five of the Tests being drawn. It was a convincing, deserved win, but Australia had not lacked chances. The seventh Test in Sydney was thrown away on the last day by poor batting when new fast bowler Dennis Lillee gave the Australian bats a reasonable target to aim for victory. This Test also led to the sacking of Bill Lawry as Australia's captain and the emergence of Ian Chappell to take his place.

The choice of Chappell as captain, has it seems, turned out to be a wise one. He took a team of raw youngsters to England in 1972 and almost grabbed the Ashes back at his first try. He might have succeeded if it had not been for the 'Yorkshire pudding' wicket at Headingley, Leeds, for the Fourth Test. Like cobras with mice, Illingworth and Derek Underwood mesmerized the Australian bats on a wicket tailor-made for spin. Australia fought back splendidly to win the Fifth Test at The Oval which squared the series two-two, thanks mainly to some gutsy batting from Paul Sheahan and wicket-keeper Rod Marsh. It was during this series, of course, that Dennis Lillee and Bob Massie developed as a pace team to be feared. Who could forget Massie's match-winning 16 wickets for 137 in the Second Test at Lord's? Ian Chappell, Greg Chappell, Sheahan, Marsh, Lillee, Massie, Stackpole, Edwards . . . yes, Australian cricket had at last thrown off the lethargy of the 1960s.

Ian Chappell

Captaining a team

Ian Michael Chappell, a stylish number three right-hand batsman, is proving one of Australia's most successful captains. He led the Australian team which drew the series against England, crushed Pakistan three–nil and then in an undefeated 15 match series in the Caribbean, beat the West Indies two–nil. In 14 appearances as captain, Chappell had seven wins, three draws and four losses, two of which were near victories.

Chappell, born in South Australia on 26 September 1943, has played 51 Tests, scoring more than 3000 runs. He is also a useful right-arm leg spinner.

So you want to be captain of your cricket team. You will need luck, ability and a sound knowledge of the game. It will help if you are something of a psychologist; but, if you are able to combine all these, there are few more rewarding facets of cricket than captaincy (regarded by many as an art).

I confess to being more mentally tired at the end of a day's play now than in the days before I started captaining teams. It is essential to put plenty of thought into every ball—not that you shouldn't when solely a player.

You never stop studying a match. What is the bowler doing? What should he be doing? What field placings should be adopted? What bowling changes should be made? What are the opposing batsmen's strengths and weaknesses?

Those questions, among many others continually exercise a captain's mind. I am a great believer in eleven heads being better than one, so I am all for a captain receiving advice from his bowlers and fieldsmen, particularly the wicket-keeper.

One of the first and most important decisions a captain has to make is what to do if he wins the toss. For me it is a difficult decision. Under Australian conditions, if I win the toss, I prefer to bat first at least ninety per cent of the time.

In club matches the weather must be considered. If it is fine on the first Saturday, you may as well bat. You never know what the next Saturday will bring. And, despite hopes of an outright win against a weaker side, first innings points are still most important. I can't stipulate any firm rules, but unless there are unusual circumstances I am happy to bat first.

Richie Benaud once told me you need luck to be a captain. Leading Australia, I seem to have a disturbing habit of losing the toss, but, in many cases they have been tosses worth losing. I would have batted first. But, although we have had to field first, often things have worked out well for us.

I think it almost goes without saying that a captain should always be capable of holding his place in the team through his ability as a batsman or bowler. The value here is that a captain can lift his side by personal example with a striking individual performance.

Knowledge of cricket can only be accumulated over a period of years. Gain experience in any way possible. Study captains and players and the way they achieve things. You are never beyond the age of learning. I like to talk with captains, and for that matter, anyone from whom I think I can learn something. Be prepared to listen, whether you are talking with a former Australian captain or the last fellow picked in a grade side.

Over the years I have tried to study players of similar types to myself to see how they go about playing the game. I rate the psychology of captaincy as extremely important. Each player in your team has a different personality, so learn to handle them.

Get to know not only the players' ability but their off-the-field personalities. This, of course, is easier to achieve on a tour when you are living together.

Field placings come with experience and your knowledge of cricket. To a certain extent you must have the courage of your convictions. Placing a field becomes easier when you get to know your bowlers and, naturally when you have good bowlers. A captain can't do much

What power and aggression. Every ounce of strength has been put into this shot by Ian Chappell as he pulls Bishen Bedi high over mid-wicket for six.

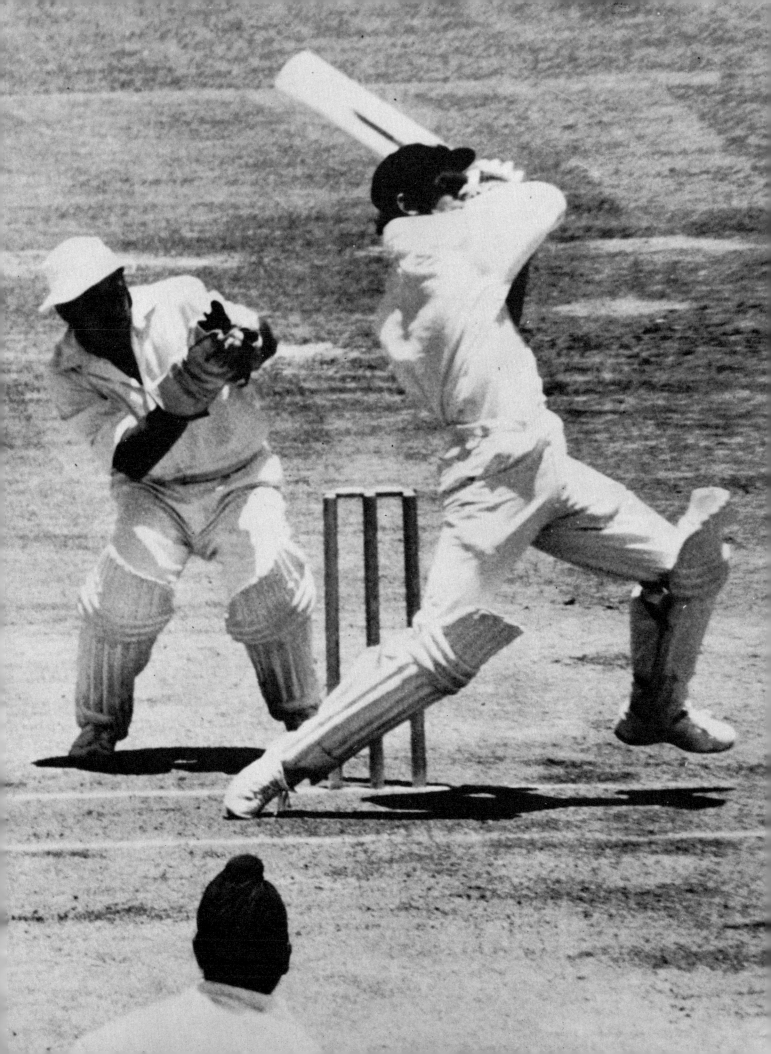

if they do not, or cannot, bowl to a particular field placement.

Deciding when to attack or tighten up again is purely a matter of learning over the years. Here is where luck can enter into it. You can be thinking of shifting a fieldsman slightly, then he takes a catch, and suddenly you are back in the game.

When placing a field, I like to let the bowler bowl to the field he wants. If I don't know much about a batsman, and the bowler does, then I let the bowler have his own way. But I still believe the captain should have the final say if there is a disagreement.

After captaining a side for some time, you get to know the fields to place for various bowlers. It's all a matter of experience. It's the captain's job to pick up the strengths and weaknesses of opposing batsmen. Where does he hit the ball most? What shots does he play convincingly? And so on.

Of course, it's the bowler's job to pick these things up, too. If a bowler is working to a plan, which he should be, he should let his captain know.

Fieldsmen can be a big help. A cover fieldsman should know if the ball is often being hit to his left. He should inform his captain. A slight adjustment would probably be necessary. A captain's task is made much easier if all players are working towards a common goal, team effort.

Generally, I place more emphasis on how to get wickets rather than how to keep the runs down. When in trouble you get to the stage where keeping the scoring rate in check is most important. But a captain's prime aim should still be to take wickets. Bait the batsman.

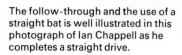

The follow-through and the use of a straight bat is well illustrated in this photograph of Ian Chappell as he completes a straight drive.

A mighty pull by Ian Chappell and the ball goes racing away through mid-wicket for another boundary.

Leave a gap in the field and encourage him to play his favourite shot.

I prefer captaining my side from first slip. I find I get a better view of the game from there, but it is a purely personal thing. Bill Lawry, for instance, preferred to station himself at mid-off or mid-on.

From first slip I find I get the batsmen's view of what the bowler is doing and the angle of the field placings. In addition, I feel I can tell when a bowler is getting tired, how hard the ball is hitting the wicket-keeper's gloves and just what the ball is doing through the air or off the pitch. When a spinner is on, I find it a great advantage to be at slip to see if his plan is working—if, in fact, he is working on one.

A captain should have some sort of liaison with his selectors, and this is one situation where I feel I have been lucky. The Australian selectors have chosen sides which, I believe, have suited my style of captaincy.

Basically, Australia has had attacking bowlers. In Dennis Lillee and Ashley Mallett we have two top-class bowlers who are not only attacking types, but are also capable of bowling for long, accurate, economic spells, always with the chance of picking up wickets. In my experience, I have found that it is not difficult to come up with ideas when your bowlers are getting wickets, but it becomes harder when two batsmen are making a lengthy stand.

I have been asked to give some hints about on-side shots. The hook and pull, of course, are the two main attacking on-side strokes. The others I regard as more for picking up runs in ones, twos and threes by making the ball work for you instead of trying to force it for fours.

It's a matter of summing up your strengths and playing within your limitations. Most batsman can hit a full toss or half-volley for four, but few can flick the ball away off their hip through the on-side for four like Greg Chappell, or, like Barry Richards, drive for four a ball which is not quite a half-volley.

The hook is a better shot to use when you are more experienced. It is a shot which I feel I play better now that I have lost the fear of its consequences. When I was young everyone told me I would get out of trying to hook. When a batsman is caught behind trying to cover-drive, he isn't told to stop cover-driving. But when he is out hooking, numerous so-called experts will tell him to stop playing the hook shot. What's the difference?

Any shot can be a prolific scorer of runs if it is played properly. Getting your feet into the right position is all-important. So, too, is learning to decide which ball should be hooked and which should be left alone. This is something with which I have had problems. It's a matter of experience and confidence.

The pull can also be a very prolific run-scoring shot and can often be used against spinners to force them to bowl a fuller length. It is one which I like to use a lot, mainly against slow bowlers.

The pull

Ian remains upright as he begins
his follow through.

Despite a full follow through, Ian
retains his balance with the help
of his upright stance.

Ashley Mallett

Off-spin bowling

Ashley Mallett, born 13 July 1945 in South Australia, is a lanky off spinner who turned down a West Indies tour in 1973 to concentrate on his profession as a journalist. Improving with age, Mallett recorded his best figures in 1972–73 in the first Test against Pakistan in Adelaide. He routed Pakistan with 8–59.

Seventeen wickets fell for only 160 runs during the third day's play of the third Test against India at Kokla Park, New Delhi on Sunday 30 November 1969. It was a black day for Australia but one of personal triumph for me. That eventful day I took 5–37, yet it was one particular bowling spell to Indian captain, the Nawab of Pataudi, which brought home to me the true value of flighting the ball.

Pataudi has only partial sight in his left eye, the legacy of a motoring accident in England. By flighting the ball above eye-level Pataudi was in difficulty. Suddenly I realised what was happening.

My mind turned back to the words of former Australian spin genius, Clarrie Grimmett: 'If you were to stand upon a bridge overlooking a motorway, it would be possible to estimate the speed of an oncoming car. Yet if you stood on the road with the same vehicle approaching at eye-level, it would be virtually impossible to judge its speed.

'The same principle is used in spin bowling.' It is far easier to detect the pitch and speed of a ball delivered at a trajectory below the level of the eye than one that is bowled at a line above eye-level.

So I proceeded to commit a Test bowler's sin. I decided to experiment for a couple of balls. I banged a couple of balls into the pitch, below eye-level all the way and spun them sharply.

Then came the crunch. . . . My next ball was a nicely flighted off-break with the perfect spinner's trajectory. The ball started just above eye-level and dropped onto a perfect length

Pataudi lunged forward and edged the ball into the waiting hands of Ian Chappell at leg slip. The Indian was not merely beaten by spin or flight, but by a combination of both. He was non-plussed as to where the ball would pitch which caused him to play well short of the ball. The spin then took the inside edge of the bat and a catch resulted.

This became my most important cricket lesson, one which I feel has had a great bearing on the general improvement in my bowling from that day on. Off-spin, as with all other types of bowling, is hard work—especially in Australian conditions. Moreover it is a challenge to succeed in spinning past the forward defensive strokes of batsmen on our flint-hard wickets.

As far as I know there is no special physique for the budding off-spinner, though it is a great advantage to have long fingers. The basic grip to bowl an off-break is to hold the ball in such a position that your forefinger and third fingers are placed as wide apart as possible across the seam.

Obviously length of fingers governs the width of spacing on the seam. The wider this spacing is the greater the leverage that is obtained and the more powerful the spin which is imparted on the ball. The ball is spun in a clockwise direction or from left to right. When the ball is delivered the back of your hand will be seen from the region of mid-off.

I advocate this grip because, with the ball spinning in the correct manner, it will hit the pitch on the seam nine times out of ten.

Always have a ball on hand at home and spin it as often as possible. The amount of break can be varied by slight variations in the bowling arm. The higher the arm action the more top-spin is imparted, and the greater the degree of bounce obtained. The lower or rounder the arm action, the more under-cut given, which means a good deal more spin but less bounce than that obtained with a high action. It is important to remember that variations in arm movements should be slight and subtle.

Ashley Mallett has tricked England opener Geoff Boycott into making a false stroke and the 'keeper has done the rest.

During practice sessions at the nets always bowl at maximum spin. Spin the ball as much as possible until you have mastered bowling on a good line and length. It is useless simply rolling your fingers over the ball hour after hour at the nets, then trying to spin the cover off the ball in a match. Not only will fingers become tired but your bowling figures will suffer. A good old-fashioned thrashing never hurt anyone, but give yourself an even chance by practising in the correct manner.

Change of pace is a most important part of the off-spinner's repertoire. Do not make the mistake of bowling too many balls round the same speed and trajectory, then proceeding to toss up a delivery much higher and slower. Batsmen will pick up an obvious change of pace easily, and quickly move into position to play a shot.

A slower ball is achieved by letting the ball go just before the normal point of delivery. It is designed to deceive a batsman into playing too early and cocking up a catch.

The quicker delivery is different in that its purpose is to deceive the batsman into playing a late shot. A batsman who tends to hit across the line of flight is a prime target for the quicker delivery. This type of indiscreet player is likely to be clean bowled or L.B.W. By letting the ball go at a point just forward of the normal point of delivery you will achieve the quicker delivery.

Often you can detect subtle changes of pace at first-class fixtures by standing at a point on the ground square of the wicket. Never forget that a batsman likes nothing better than facing a bowler who is stereotyped—a bowler who tends to bowl every ball at a similar pace and flight. A mixture of pace and flight is essential for an off-spinner to succeed in our Australian conditions. It is often the difference between a really good spinner and a run-of-the-mill trundler.

Using the crease is another important aspect of off-spinning. A continual change in the angle the ball is bowled to a batsman adds to his problems in countering your bowling. Changing the angle of delivery is quite simple. All you do is bowl one ball close to the stumps, then another a couple of inches further out on the bowling crease. The closer to the stumps you bowl, the greater is the angle of trajectory away from the batsman. The further you deliver from the non-striker's stumps on the crease, the greater angle of in-slant becomes.

I bowl more deliveries close to the stumps for a particular reason. It gives me a slight away-curve and break-back. A batsman is often deceived into leaving a large gap between bat

Ashley Mallett in action at the nets, sending down one of his slow spinners.

One that got through the leg-trap. Ashley Mallett glances between wicket-keeper Alan Knott and Basil D'Oliviera at short leg.

Field Placement

Off-spinner to a right-hander on a turning wicket

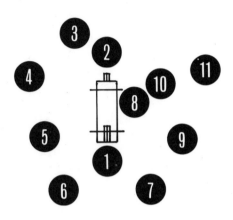

1. Bowler	7. Mid-on
2. Wicket-keeper	8. Short forward leg
3. Slip	9. Mid-wicket
4. Point	10. Short forward silly leg
5. Cover	11. Square leg
6. Mid-off	

The two forward short legs are the potential dangers to batsmen. It is advisable to bowl around the wicket if the turn is 16 cm or more. Fieldsmen can be altered accordingly by pushing some out and replacing them with a short leg.

Don't be in a hurry to do this on a real 'turner' as it is only a matter of a few balls before another ball will be hit into a player's pads and rebound into the air.

The more fieldsmen in catching positions, the better.

Off-spinner to a right-hander on a good wicket

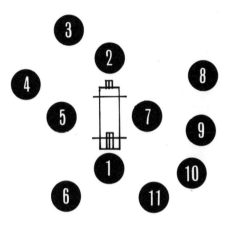

1. Bowler	7. Forward short leg
2. Wicket-keeper	8. Backward square leg
3. First slip	9. Forward square leg
4. Point	10. Mid-wicket
5. Cover	11. Mid-on
6. Mid-off	

Even on a good wicket it is important to begin with an attacking field. Always start with this basic field on such a wicket. If the ball doesn't turn a great deal and you find the batsman is on top, you can change the field by pushing back the forward short leg and dropping number 9 back on the fence.

Ashley Mallett bowls to Brian Reynolds of Northamptonshire, drawing him well forward with a ball flighted and spinning.

and pad when he follows the away-curve, but he fails to cover the spin off the wicket. The commonly-used term 'bowled through the gate' usually occurs in this manner with an off-spinner operating.

Once again I cannot stress too much the need to be subtle in changing the angle of delivery by using different points on the bowling crease. Here, subtle means to move your feet only a matter of inches on the crease.

On a wicket which is conducive to a lot of spin it is to your advantage to bowl around the wicket. There is a greater angle of away-swerve—which really is merely the greater angle of release point—and the spin straightens the ball back onto the line of the stumps. A ball pitched on off-stump and spun sharply would most likely hit off or middle stump if the batsman missed. An umpire is also more likely to uphold an L.B.W. decision on such a wicket while you operate around the wicket.

One ball of importance which I have not mentioned up till now is the top-spinner. For this delivery, grip the ball on the shiny surface. Your fingers are still placed wide apart but they are not to touch any part of the seam. The top-spinner is used mainly for variety and is useful for letting a batsman know you do not merely spin the ball into his pads. A good tactical move against a new batsman on a turning wicket is to bowl two or three top-spinners, then toss him up a vicious off-break.

Tactics play an important part in the game as you cannot hope to succeed as an off-spinner in big cricket without the combination of brains and ability. The off-spinner must be able to bowl with extreme accuracy to put any plan into action.

If a player is continually playing forward and striking the ball on the half-volley, you are bowling too far up. It could well be that you are not spinning the ball enough or that your trajectory is too flat. Remember that the trajectory must be just above the level of the eyes for all your deliveries except the faster one. It goes without saying that if a player is con-sistently playing off the back foot your bowling is far too short.

Try to evaluate the batsman's weaknesses. Should he tend to hit with the spin in the region of mid-on and mid-wicket there is a good chance he will become over-confident. Bowl three or four off-breaks and let him hit them on the on-side then bowl him up a top-spinner. If he attempts to hit this ball on the on side he will in fact be hitting across the line of flight. A catch at slip may well result.

Experience will teach you many things about tactics but, I repeat, without the ability to spin the ball well on a good line and length, no plan will ever succeed. You do not have to be a University graduate to become a good cricket tactician. To be a really good spin bowler you need to have sufficient commonsense to be able to know when to bowl your top-spinner or when to bowl around the wicket.

Watch as many Sheffield Shield matches and Test games as you can and as the off-spinner is bowling, try to think out the batsman with him. It can be a lot of fun and you'll obtain great satisfaction from the game if you think along with the bowler. You may get to the stage where you'll be saying to yourself: 'For Pete's sake, bowl him the top-spinner; he's hitting across the line or with the off-spin.'

Off-spin bowling, as with all facets of cricket, is a side-on game. At delivery the body should be side-on to the batsman. The left arm should be well up and the back foot parallel to the bowling crease. Your eyes should look over the left shoulder at a spot on the wicket where you intend pitching the ball. From here you move into the actual releasing of the ball by trans-ferring your weight to the front foot. Total body weight is on the front foot at the moment of delivery and the left leg should be braced and perfectly straight.

Finally, no off-spinner can do well without plenty of practice. Richie Benaud is the best example I can think of in this regard. Benaud became the best leg-spinner in the World in his time, by constant practice. Throughout the summer months he would bowl for hours at a cap placed on a good length in an empty S.C.G. net.

To all the budding off-spinners in Australia, I wish the best of luck.

Dennis Lillee

Leading the attack

The point of delivery. Dennis Lillee is high in the air as he strives for that little extra in pace and bounce.

Dennis Keith Lillee rocketed to stardom on the 1972 tour of England. He took 31 wickets in the five Tests, a record for an Australian bowler in England. His sustained speed and sharp lift made him hard for opposing batsmen to play. Lillee's best figures came during a World XI series in Australia during the 1971–72 season when he took 8–29 Serious back trouble ruined his tour of the West Indies in 1973. Born in Perth, Western Australia on 18 July 1949, Lillee still has time to recover and take many more wickets.

I don't hate batsmen . . . I just like to get them out quickly and for as low a score as possible. This is a bowler's task. If an opening bowler can get two or three quick wickets, he has done his job. If he can also pick up a couple more wickets, he has done an especially good job. This is how I play the game. You can't be kind to a batsman. He is there trying to hit you for four and you are there to get him out.

I think co-ordination is possibly the most important thing for a fast bowler to possess. People often ask the question: why is one bowler faster than another? It's hard trying to put a finger on the reason. Really it is like any sport. Like sprinting for example. Why can one man beat another of similar size and build over a given distance? Usually it is because his co-ordination is better.

Basically a fast bowler should be of reasonable height, but he should not be muscle-bound. Take John Snow, the English fireball. There's nothing menacing about him until he takes a cricket ball into his hand. In fact, he is surprisingly lithe for a fast bowler. He's tall enough but when you look at his whippet-like body you wonder how he manages to bowl as fast as he does. Snow makes use of all his physical attributes and, with his wonderful co-ordination, can terrify most players.

The length of a fast bowler's run-up is tremendously important. When I was playing at school in under-age matches I'm sure it was my run-up which frightened batsmen more than my pace. But when you start climbing up the cricket ladder a long run-up is really of little consequence—unless you can bowl fast too!

Your run-up should be only as long as it need be. You should be at maximum pace about four strides before your delivery stride. If you can accomplish this off a fifteen metre run-up, fine. I run about twentyfive metres to reach this pace and to be ready for each delivery.

It is important for a fast bowler to realise that he shouldn't try to bowl every delivery at break neck speed. I recall doing just that when I first started playing cricket, thus wearing myself out too quickly.

Variation is an important thing for a fast bowler to learn. He should start bowling from his normal delivery position, where his front foot lands on the batting crease. If, during a particular game, he is bowling successfully and getting wickets from this orthodox position, he would be well advised to persevere with this method.

But if a batsman gets on top, it's time for a change. One of the things a bowler *can* do is change the angle of delivery. This happened in a Sheffield Shield match with Western Australia against Victoria. I had been bowling from the usual position to Alan Seiler. Then I sent one down from a different place—coming in from a much wider angle, further away from the stumps. It was enough to confuse Seiler and he snicked the ball and was caught behind. Although the ball did not swing at all, the different angle presented to the batsman caused his downfall.

Pace can be varied. Bowl some fast balls, then whip in a medium-pace delivery and you can force a player to mistime the ball. A catch forward of the wicket may be the result.

Surprise is another—in the fast bowler's bag of tricks. A typical example of this can be taken from the same Sheffield Shield game between Western Australia and Victoria. Ian Redpath was the batsman and he had belted me and the other Western Australia bowlers to all points of the MCG compass.

As I have said, I usually run-off about twenty-five metres, and 'Redders' was expecting the same. On this occasion, however, I turned and started to run in from about six or seven metres. Naturally enough, he wasn't properly ready. He stopped, started to take guard, paused again and then saw that I was going to bowl seriously from the shortened run-up. I whizzed it down as fast as I could from that distance and 'Redders' touched a neat little catch to John Inverarity at first slip.

Of course these variations may not always work, but you will notice, once you try a few, that the batsman starts to think twice about the next delivery. Once you have a batsman in two minds you are getting closer to gaining his wicket.

Fast bowling has its rewards, but it can be backbreaking and disillusioning. Anybody concerned about hard work shouldn't even dream of taking it up.

A fast bowler will always suffer from some ache or pain. He may get tired in the legs, his back might hurt or he may just suffer from getting more sweat in his eyes than any other player. It's no easy life, believe me. The test of a fast bowler's mettle is usually on his ability to overcome these nagging problems.

The fast, rising ball can be difficult to counter, as Sunil Gavaskar, of India, found on this occasion. He couldn't get his bat out of the way in time and just touched this delivery from Lillee which was caught by the keeper.

Fitness is another of the prime requisites. If you want to eat rice pudding and cream pie all your life, then you're not cut out to bowl fast.

A bowler must be prepared to work and work hard, not just in a game, but at the nets and then away from the nets doing extra running. After I finish my net practice I work until I can't blow out the flame of a candle . . . then do some more.

Of course you don't do this sort of hard stuff when you're in the middle of a game, but pre-season. Between matches you've got to be prepared to do the work that will give you the stamina to bowl in the face of great odds.

After pace, the next most important thing in a fast bowler's make-up is direction. It's all right to be able to scare a batsman, but if the direction is missing so then will your share of the wickets be missing.

This was one of my big problems when I first broke into first-class cricket. I was quick enough, but the direction wasn't there. It can be taken from this that direction will always improve with experience, but it's this lack of direction that has been the unsettling of many good young players who might have developed into top-class fast bowlers.

One of the shock weapons of the fast bowler is, of course, the 'bumper' or 'bouncer'. But there are bouncers and bouncers. A bad one just isn't worth the effort. In top-class cricket a bad bouncer will usually be dispatched, special delivery, to the boundary. If it goes on the full then it's six and this is the sort of thing that will lead your captain to replace you in the attack. And if you are not bowling, you can't take wickets.

There are times when you don't bowl bouncers—and there are players you don't bounce; for example, on a MCG wicket to Victorian opener, Keith Stackpole. I won't bounce 'Stacky' on a dead wicket. In fact it's rather stupid to bounce any good player on a wicket that's not giving you any help. As soon as the ball has gone, you know you've made a mistake. It crunches into the fence, loses a bit of shine—and there are four more runs against your name as a reminder that bowling short didn't get you a wicket.

But the correctly aimed 'bouncer' bowled on the right sort of wicket is a more than useful weapon.

Like most cricketers I was terribly impressed at an early age by the greats of my youth . . . and of the past. I used to watch and try to copy them all. Alan Davidson, Graham McKenzie, Wes Hall . . . these were the players who impressed me when I was a lad.

Since then I have had the opportunity to talk to and, most important, to listen to other former fast bowling greats. I've had chats with Keith Miller, Ray Lindwall, Alan Davidson and others, and they have all helped at some stage along the line. I think it's wise to listen to all the advice you can get.

Apart from this, probably the only other requirement you'll need is a little bit of luck. Take a player like Garth McKenzie. There's a player who bowled magnificently for his State and country, usually without much luck at all. I think he had more catches dropped off his bowling than most and it was during one of his spells of outs that I learnt another important thing: if luck is against you, batsmen are playing and missing and catches are going down, you've got to stick with it. This is a very necessary lesson to learn, and the quicker you learn it the better player you will be. Bad luck never seemed to upset Garth. He just kept plugging away.

A fast bowler is usually only as good as his fielding side. Those catches can mean the difference between finishing with good figures or bad ones. If the catches are dropped, you must keep trying.

Give up at any stage and you're admitting defeat. A good fast bowler is never defeated!

Dennis Lillee gets some of his own medicine. Here he ducks a bumper, like the batsmen duck from him at times.

Fast bowling

Dennis Lillee uses this leap before his final stride to help him gain momentum. Keeping his eyes on his target, Dennis' left elbow is being raised to catapult him into his delivery stride.

The delivery stride. Dennis uses his left arm to propel himself. Notice his eyes have not left his target.

With accuracy vital, Dennis still watches his target over his left shoulder. He is almost completely side-on and ready to thrust himself into delivery.

The moment of release. Dennis'
left shoulder dips and he is ready
to deliver the ball front on. He gets
the best result by bowling from
the highest point of his delivery
action.

Even on the follow-through Dennis
has his eyes steadfastly on his target.
A lesson to all bowlers.

Paul Sheahan

Fielding and cover driving

Paul Sheahan, a dashing right-hand batsman, celebrated his newly found concentration and fluency with 1000 runs in the Australian season of 1972–73.

Born in Victoria on 30 September 1946, Sheahan helped Australia to draw the 1972 series in England with two fighting innings that announced him as a power. He thrashed all bowlers on his return to Australia and cherished his new role as an opening batsman.

A 'certainty' for a tour of the West Indies, Sheahan surprised the cricketing world when he made himself unavailable for the 1973 tour because of his teaching commitments.

Sheahan is an outstanding asset to any side as he is one of the world's swiftest and surest cover-fieldsmen.

There is a basic principle in any ball sport . . . keep your eye on the ball. It applies in golf, tennis, table tennis, football—and equally in cricket. It is essential when both batting and fielding, and unless you obey the golden rule you have no chance of success.

Let's concentrate on fielding first. It is a major part of cricket, and in some games players, if they don't bowl and then miss a bat, are involved only in fielding. So, sometimes, fielding can be your whole contribution to the team's efforts. And you can't let your team down.

Fielding is something that a player can teach himself, develop on his own and improve through practice. One of the most difficult aspects of fielding is that you have to concentrate on every ball. It's vital. You may have only one opportunity for a catch or run-out in the complete day's play; and it can be missed by lost concentration on just one delivery. That moment of dreaming could cost your side the match. So it is therefore easy to see why con-centration is so important—every ball of the innings.

One way of improving your concentration in the field is to assess the strengths and weaknesses of the opposing batsman, calculate how you would contain him, and be determined to stop everything that comes your way.

You should take fielding as a personal challenge. You against the batsman. If he hits the ball your way, you have to cut it off, return it and deprive him of as many runs as possible.

Outfieldsmen must always move in with the bowler. This is an asset as your body is then in motion, making it easier to accelerate quickly after a ball. It is the same as in golf. Golfers press forward slightly before starting their swings, thus setting their body in motion to get full use of their shot.

Fielding in the covers is a difficult task as you have such a wide area to patrol and are generally facing hard-hit deliveries. But I enjoy working there because I have developed a one-handed pick-up and throw. That's essential for any cover fieldsman. You must be able to pick up a ball and return it without jerking—it has to be one smooth action.

It is also important to learn to pick up a ball side-on. Running sidewards and picking up the ball to return to the 'keeper is about ninety per cent of cover-fielding. Doing this, and and quickly at that, can often make a batsman think twice about taking a single. That's another run saved!

You must also learn to throw the ball from a standing position, rather than depend on a running start. The top fieldsmen will pick up the ball just inside the boundary and, apparently without looking, let fly. They would waste valuable seconds if they had to turn around and run for several paces before hurling in the return.

It's all practice. You can practise accuracy by throwing a tennis ball at the dust-bin in the back yard . . . at a particular brick on a wall . . . at the clothesline. And instead of standing behind the nets at practice, get together a few mates and a stump and throw in returns.

Paul Sheahan sweeps elegantly down to the fine leg fence. He has gone down on one knee to secure maximum control of the ball.

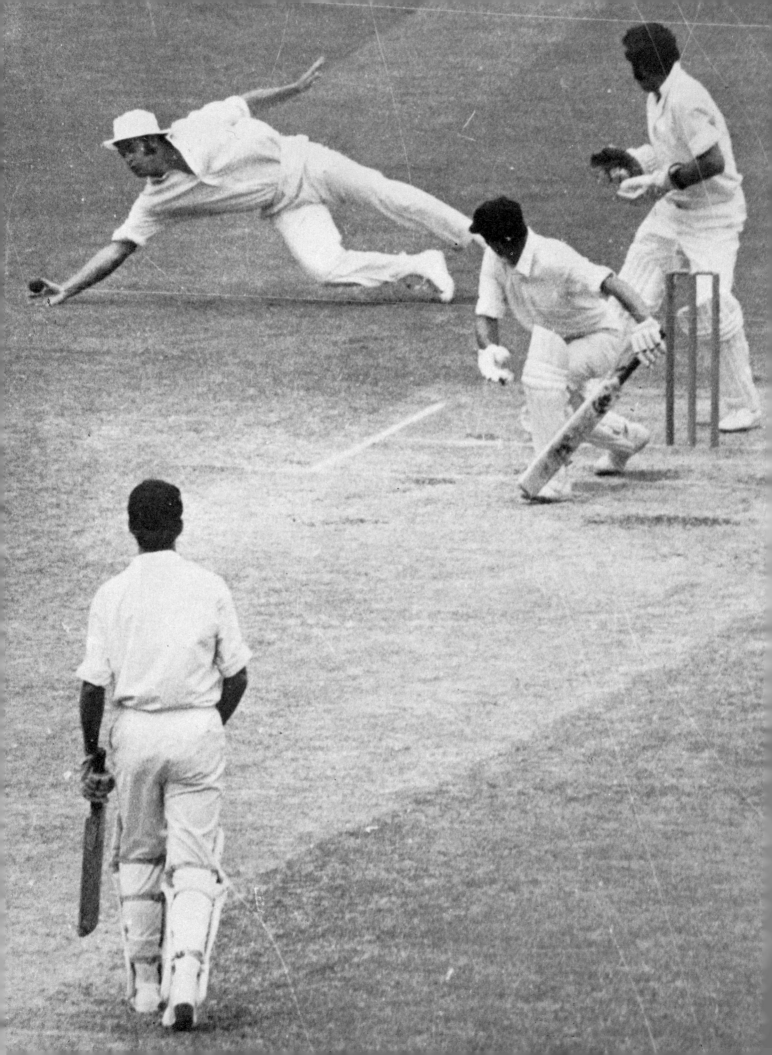

You will never be a perfect fieldsman. There never has been one and never will be. But you can always improve and gain confidence in your own ability.

I have always believed confidence is a big part of fielding. If you don't think you can stop a hard-hit ball, more than likely you won't. You must develop the attitude that you can stop anything that comes your way, no matter how fast, how hard.

Anticipation is another skill that will improve your fielding. When in the covers it is a good move to watch the batsman's actions. By watching the way he moves his feet into a particular position, you can get a fair idea where the ball is going.

Paul Sheahan is one of the most stylish players in the game as he shows with this forcing shot through the off-side field.

A catch that wasn't. This ball, from the edge of Doug Walters' bat, flew to Hilton Ackerman at first slip. He grasped it—then grassed it.

The best piece of fielding I have ever seen came from West Indies star, Clive Lloyd. Ibadulla drove to covers like a bullet and strode down the wicket fully convinced it was four. Clive threw himself to his right, and in one action, while still in mid-air, had the ball back to the 'keeper with Ibadulla out of his ground. His movement was so fast that I am sure he had not hit the ground before the 'keeper had the bails off. It was unbelievable!

Clive has the assets that every cricketer should strive for in his fielding. He is agile, fast, and can return a ball accurately, powerfully and in double time. And he is fit. Every fieldsman should be fit.

Fitness helps you see out a long day in the field, and stick to the task with enthusiasm and energy. Tiredness can never be an excuse for poor fielding, even late in the day. Neither should you blame a long hard day in the field for your batting failure. If you have to bat late in the day, either as an opener or as a night-watchman, there is no room for tiredness.

Always remember with fielding that you can save many runs by being alert, enthusiastic and fit. A top fieldsman, especially in the covers, can cut off up to fifty runs by his sharpness. That's fifty runs less your side has to chase.

Batting is similar to throwing. If your body is in the correct position it should be 'all systems go'.

I think the cover-drive is one of the most graceful and effective shots in the book. That is, when it is played correctly. The cover drive requires your feet and body to be in the right position, because no matter what else you do, it won't come off unless they are.

It is vital that you select the right ball to cover-drive. You should never attempt one to a ball pitched on line with the stumps, or one too wide outside the off.

Irrespective of what drive you play, your back-lift must be straight. For a cover-drive, your front foot must be in line with the spot you want the ball to go to, and the back-lift straight.

One vital fact that many people forget is that your forward shoulder must also be in the direction you want the ball to go. Then you must go through with the shot. Once you have made up your mind to play a cover-drive, play it. Don't pull the shot or you run the risk of being caught, either from a snick behind or by 'lollying' a catch in the mid-wicket area. Again, as in fielding, you must be confident you can play the cover-drive. And confidence comes only from practice.

The sweep

With eyes fixed firmly on the ball, Ian is ready to play the stroke. The bat is still swinging on the down slope, and to ensure the ball will go directly to ground Ian is ready to roll his wrists.

On contact the wrists are rolled. Notice the ball is heading directly to ground. The rolling of the wrist is helped by keeping a stiff right arm, as Ian shows clearly here.

Notice Ian's control of balance. He helped play a good stroke and keep his balance by keeping his legs firmly in the original position shown in frame 1.

Keith Stackpole

Opening the batting, playing the fast bowling

Keith Raymond Stackpole, born in Melbourne on 7 October 1942, became a self-made opening batsman and Australia's vice-captain and made a success of both jobs with his aggressive style. He retired after the 1974 New Zealand tour.

Stackpole has been the scourge of England. In Australia in 1971–72 he was the only batsman to handle the short-pitched deliveries and returned an average of 52.25. Then in England in 1972 he topped the run aggregate with 1 309 at an average of 46.63. He was also the highest scorer in Tests with 485 runs at an average of 53.88.

His consistency was a major asset. In England in 1972, he had ten Test innings for one century and five scores over 50.

A useful wrist spinner, Stackpole was rated one of the best slips fieldsmen in the world.

Opening the batting is not simply a matter of walking out and letting fly. There are many things an opener must do if he is to capably and conscientiously live up to the responsible role he has been chosen to fill.

The opener must get his team off to a good start. If he fails, often, so does the side. It is remarkable how many times a batting collapse will follow the failure of one or both openers.

So let's take the 'musts' in order.

First of all you have to adjust to the weather—and that means, primarily, wind and light. Wind is important because one of the fast bowler's principal weapons will be his ability to swing the new ball. The opening batsman, therefore, will need to know what sort of swing

This shot from Keith Stackpole, off Pakistani spinner and captain, Intikhab Alam, went for six.

35

bowler he is facing, whether he swings mostly in or away, if the swing is late and sharp. With this knowledge, which he should have before he even steps onto the ground, the opening batsman must then adapt it to the weather of the day. If the wind is strong enough to assist the bowler, then the batsman must calculate the effect it will have on his batting, bearing in mind how the opposing bowler is likely to use it.

Light is not so complicated. Basically it is a matter of getting used to the strength of light so that the sudden transition from the relative darkness of the dressingroom to the glare of the mid-oval area does not cause a batsman to lose the flight of the ball.

There's one more factor to attend to before taking strike; that is, the placing of the field. An opening batsman does not have the advantage of being able to observe these placements as his colleagues will be able to do while they sit and wait their turn. He must memorise the men and their positions in the few seconds he has while the field is being set.

For instance, it is vital to know if there is a man at deep square leg or another at leg slip. And it's not good enough to know roughly where they are. If there is someone at deep square leg, you must know how far in from the fence he is and whether he is a good fieldsman. It will be necessary to establish, early, whether he moves quickly and how fast and accurately he can throw. That man in the deep can mean early singles to the opening batsman. This is so important because an opener can, very early, break up a field by patting or glancing the ball away on the leg side and moving through for one. This sort of thing has an upsetting effect on a fielding side and can force them onto the defensive very early. But these tactics cannot be undertaken successfully unless that glance is kept well away from a leg-slip fieldsman, if he is in that position.

So now the stage is set and the opening batsman must take strike and get on with the job. Of course he must not take risks but, at the same time, he must not let the day get away on him. Making runs is what this game of cricket is all about and that is what he must set about doing.

For my part, I like to do the attacking myself. This sort of approach has its advantages for an opener because, mostly, the bowlers will set their fields close to the pitch which means that a ball hit with any power at all should be able to get past them—and that means runs. A hard hit delivery in the early stages is usually four. Later on, when the field deepens, that same shot may be worth only one.

A typical Stackpole swing, with plenty of beef in it. And the ball goes speeding away to the boundary.

But there are disadvantages, too. Like facing fearsome 'quickies' who are fresh, have a new ball in their hand and one idea in their heads— to get you out. Facing Dennis Lillee or John Snow is no piece of cake. They are fast, and I mean really fast. Confidence plays a big part here. You always have to remember that you are playing the same standard of cricket as the bowler, and he has just as many problems as you.

An attacking attitude to any loose deliveries can give a batsman almost immediate ascendancy.

A couple of good shots early and the bowler has something to think about. He might have

Keith Stackpole practising at the nets and hitting the ball right in the middle of the bat.

art of playing only the shots of which he was complete master made him a great player, a great opening batsman. Bobby developed the cover-drive to his advantage, but used it sparingly.

Every opening batsman must have a good array of strokes and should never depend on one stroke. I have earned a reputation as a savage hooker of the ball and any bowler I come up against knows this. Bowlers are not stupid, so they don't feed you your good strokes.

In my latter first class innings I was not getting many bouncers and so I had been driving more. If I depended solely or mainly on my hook I would not make many runs. You have to be able to hit the ball with any shot, although obviously you have favourite ones.

Being aggressive does not mean trying to hit every ball to the fence. In any big score about thirty per cent of the runs come in singles. Batsmen should always be prepared to take the single as it has two definite advantages.

First and foremost, it adds to your score in the same way as a six or a four. Maybe not as fast, but the runs are still coming and that's the main thing.

Secondly, a single can be a weapon against the bowler. It gives both batsmen a chance to face the bowler, and often he will have to change his line or length to the different styles of each. This can be upsetting to the bowler and, unconsciously, the batsman has him thinking seriously.

Now let's get down to batting itself. There are two basic fundamentals, and these apply especially to opening batsmen against a new ball.

Play each ball on its merits.

Play leg–to–leg and off–to–off.

They are simple rules but crucial to success.

Playing each ball on its merits is the basic way to stay at the crease. You have to keep the good balls out and hit the loose deliveries hard.

Never under estimate your opponent. Just because he bowls a loose delivery outside the off one ball, it doesn't mean he will bowl another the following ball. This is a trap for many players. They hit a ball for four, and are firmly on top of the situation. Then for some strange reason they try to hit every ball to the fence.

That style quickly sees the batsman back in the pavilion while another batsman is calmly hitting the bowler all over the field. It only takes one good ball, which you don't play on its merits, and you are out of the game.

Leg–to–leg and off–to–off is something

to change his length or direction and so the tension is broken. You are on top . . . but you have to stay there.

And the way to stay there is to play only shots over which you have complete control. Former Australian captain and opener Bob Simpson was a perfect example of what I mean.

I can hardly remember seeing Bobby playing a cover drive to the fence. If he did play that shot (one of his less effective shots) he would play it for two or maybe three. It was not his strongest shot so he guided it rather than tried to hit the cover off the ball.

But balls on the leg side were quickly and repeatedly dispatched to the boundary. That everyone should learn from the time they first pick up a bat. If a ball travels down the leg side, hit it to leg. If it is directed outside the off stump, hit it to off. It's as simple as that.

Likewise, if a ball is on the stumps it should go straight back. The 'ideal' example is when a straight ball is pitched well up on middle stump. The ball should be hit straight back and hit the middle stump at the bowler's end.

In other words, cross-bat shots are OUT!

Besides the two fundamentals and confidence, there are two vital ingredients needed by an opening batsman.

Concentration is one. It's difficult, but an opening batsman, particularly, must discipline himself to think of nothing else except wearing down those bowlers and getting runs at the same time.

The other 'ingredient' is decision. An opener must be decisive. Against fast bowlers he just can't afford to be changing his mind, or his stroke. He simply doesn't have the time. Make up your mind once and stay with that decision. Either you play forward or you play back. There is no room for an in-between sort of shot.

Now, a few tips on hooking. This is an instinct shot, a reflex action. If you get a bouncer, you either hook or you duck. That too is a decisive action. Never try to hook a ball that is bouncing too high. Likewise let bouncers wide down the off side pass through harmlessly.

The only bouncers to hook are those down the leg side or those over the stumps. And if you want to keep your head on your shoulders, take this advice.

When getting in a position to hook, the back foot *must* always go back towards the *off* stump. If your leg moves towards the leg stump, or anywhere but the *off* stump, you cannot get inside the ball. So you run the risk of being hit on the head.

I have occasionally been criticised for getting out on the hook shot, but that is normal. To be caught from a hook shot is to be criticised for being unorthodox. If you are bowled, LBW or caught behind you are almost pardoned.

Hooking is a shot that can be dismissed from a batsman's repertoire. But what good would that do for me? I wouldn't score as many runs as I do now. I like exciting cricket and the hook is the most exciting shot in the book.

Playing the cut shot is similar to hooking. If you are going to cut, play only the balls outside the off stump. You can get your weight over deliveries outside off stump, and so you don't run the risk of leaning back for the shot and being caught behind.

You can teach yourself to be an opening

batsman. I did. I followed these points:

Play each ball on its merits.

Apply one hundred per cent concentration.

Play only the shots of which you are complete master.

Be decisive in playing either forward or back.

Play leg–to–leg or off–to–off.

Be confident.

Don't be intimidated by 'quickies'.

And most of all, have an aggressive outlook.

Keith Stackpole is perfectly balanced, a picture of power and grace, as he plays this shot.

Another boundary to Stackpole as he hits the ball firmly past square leg.

The square cut

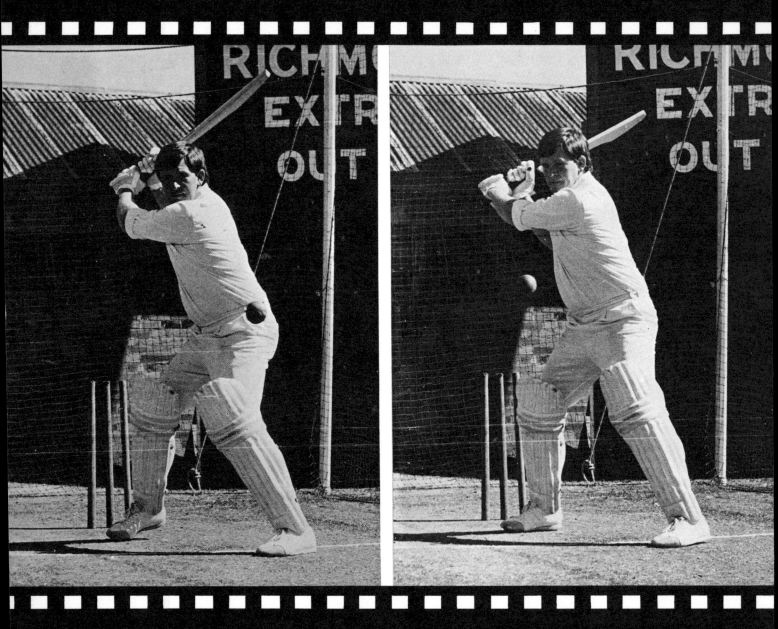

Keith Stackpole is a strong player of the square cut. He ensures correct position by moving his right foot well back and across his stumps. This allows him more

Keith retains an upright position to help him hit over the ball.

Crack ! Keith gains added power
by transferring his body weight
onto his right foot, thus letting
him 'lay into the ball'. Notice on
contact the bat is on the down-
ward slant, to help hit the ball into
the ground. Notice, also, that he
has hit the ball right in the centre
of the bat.

Keith ensures the safety of the
stroke by rolling his wrists. By
'laying into the ball' instead of
pulling away on contact, Keith
gained more power.

Bob Massie

Swinging the ball

Robert Arnold Lockyer Massie rewrote the record books on the English tour of 1972 with 16–137 (8–84 and 8–53) in his Test debut at Lord's. It was the third best-ever performance in Test cricket history. Born on 14 April 1947, Massie has been plagued by injury in his cricket career. He played four out of five Tests in England, two out of three against Pakistan in Australia during 1972–73, and struggled for a match in the West Indies.

Not renowned for his batting, Massie became a hero against Pakistan in the Third Test in Sydney in 1973 when he scored 42 to push Australia to victory.

One of the strangest things I've found about playing Test cricket is that often I have found myself bowling to men I have almost worshipped as cricketers. Like that day in Melbourne. I had the ball in my hand and was nearly ready to run in when I found I had to really concentrate on the job at hand.

The bloke down the other end of the wicket with his bat quietly tapping away at the crease was none other than . . . Gary Sobers. How can I get *him* out? This is the thought that kept coming back to me.

Well, I figured, rather than frustrate myself before I've even started, I must try to frustrate him by bowling a good line and length.

And this is what swing bowling is all about—line and length. Achieve these and the wickets will come.

Of course, bowling only a cut above medium pace you must have the ability to move the ball around a bit too, but with swing it's important that you don't try to bowl the batsman out. Let the ball do the work for you.

This was pointed out to me unforgettably that day as I bowled to Sobers, who was then playing for the Rest of the World. I concentrated solely on line and length. If you don't,

against a player of his calibre, you will be pasted all over the field.

My first ball to Sobers was cracked for four, but then a tight, engrossing struggle developed between us. Shortly afterwards I moved one away and he narrowly missed getting a touch to the 'keeper. With that delivery in the back of my mind I bowled him a few in-swingers. He handled these all right, but the next out-swinger he faced he did get that touch and was out.

Bowling to Sobers that day taught me three things.

First, to concentrate.

Secondly, not to try to bowl a player out by bowling too fast.

Thirdly, that it is possible to plot a batsman's downfall.

Oh, there's more to it than that. But it is most important to keep those points foremost in your mind.

In any phase of cricket you have to be on the job from the time you walk on to the ground. If you are a bowler you should have a good knowledge of the batsmen you are to bowl at. Where possible you should know of any weakness the batsman has so you can work on this weakness to get him where you want him—back in the pavilion.

More often than not—particularly when the wickets aren't coming—swing bowlers fall into a spider's web by trying to bowl too fast. On the 1972–73 Western Australian tour of the Eastern States I continually found myself so worried about not getting a wicket that I tried to put too much into my bowling. Consequently I lost my length, line and swing, the wickets didn't come and by the end of the day's play the scoreboard nearly always told a pretty sorry tale for me.

A swing bowler must let the ball do the work for him. Put too much into it and you're dead. I'm not suggesting that fast bowlers should heed this advice, but swing bowling is a delicate affair and this is how it should be approached.

When I say that a bowler can plot a batsman's downfall, I don't mean he sits there like Rommel on a campaign in the North African desert. But it is certainly possible to carefully construct an over, planning to get his wicket

Bob Massie is all concentration and poise as he prepares to send down one of his swingers.

on a particular ball. This is where those two Ls—line and length—come in again, because if they are not there, it's impossible to know if you're going to get a wicket at all.

But, like anything else, swing bowling must have a start and it's this start to a career as a bowler that is probably more important than anything else.

Once you've found your niche in cricket it's important that you put the necessary hours into your game to improve. Nothing in life, particularly sport these days, comes easily. A young cricketer must be prepared to work, and bowlers usually work harder than most.

As a young bloke, I spent hours plugging away at the nets, concentrating for the entire session on my bowling. Do enough of this and your legs will grow strong enough to bowl long spells in any conditions. Also your breathing will improve to a standard necessary to be able to think about bowling rather than how you will keep going.

Even at the nets Bob Massie puts everthing into his delivery as this fine, close-up photograph shows.

Of course, most swing bowlers will come into the wind. This must be used so that it is turned into a benefit, rather than a handicap.

But let's get down to basics. The first thing with swing bowling is to find out whether or not you can swing the ball. Surprisingly enough some players, even shown the correct way to hold the ball for in-swing and out-swing, still can't move the ball sufficiently to worry a batsman.

This is the basic grip for the in-swinger . . . the ball is held with the shine on the opposite side you want the ball to go, with the seam pointing to leg slip. The arm follow through is down, and cut away from the body.

The use of the in-swinger will depend entirely on conditions. If the breeze is more suitable for out-swingers, the in-swinger may be used very sparingly, more as a shock delivery. In normal conditions, the in-swinger is probably used best as a surprise ball, when the batsman has become accustomed to the out-swingers.

The out-swinger is the swing bowler's most important delivery. It is held with the seam pointing to first slip. In the bowling action, the arm follow through is cut across the body. This ball, in fact, would get about seventy per cent of the swing bowler's wickets when the batsman snicks the ball to the 'keeper or the slips field.

In England during 'that' Test match when I got sixteen wickets, most of them were from the out-swinger with catches going behind the wicket.

Conditions are best for swing bowlers when it's humid and overcast, with a slight breeze. But more often than not you must be prepared to bowl in conditions that don't suit. It could well be a hot, still day, with the ball hardly moving at all. In these conditions other elements, like an economical run-up, will play a big part in just how long you are able to stay in the attack.

A swing bowler's action should be economical. Even a swing bowler can develop a bouncer. Of course, bowling at medium pace you must be careful when to use it, otherwise you'll find you are just presenting a good batsman with four runs. But if the batsman is aware that you can bowl a good bouncer, this will always be in the back of his mind and he will naturally adopt a little more caution against your bowling.

But bowling, whether it be swing or pace, spells plenty of hard work, disappointment, sweat, sore muscles . . . and success. Success is what we're all after—and we won't be let down provided we're prepared to work, be disappointed, sweat and put up with sore muscles.

The cover drive

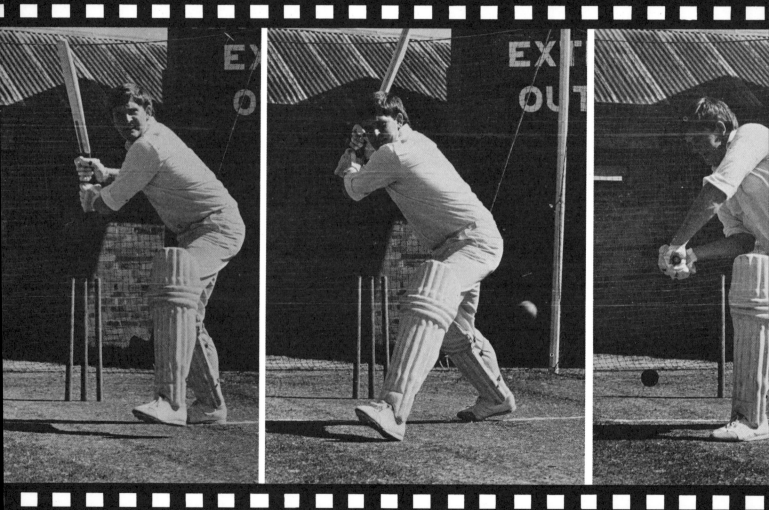

Greg Chappell

The perfectionist

Gregory Stephen Chappell is a world-class batsman. He made a fine entry into Test cricket by scoring 108 runs at his debut at Perth, becoming the eleventh Australian to achieve this feat. That was against England in 1970.

Two years later he toured England and returned with the second highest tour aggregate of 1260 runs at an average of 70. In the five Tests he scored 437 runs at an average of 48.55, including two centuries. The tour made him a Wisden's Cricketer of the Year.

Younger brother of Ian, Greg Chappell was born at Glenelg, South Australia, on 7 August 1948. He is a useful right-arm medium pacer and a brilliant close-in fieldsman.

One of the great attractions of cricket is its ability to produce so many players of varying styles. Rarely do you find two the same.

But the successful cricketers, and in this case batsmen, all follow certain basic fundamentals around which their game is developed. Generalising, they boil down to technique, footwork and concentration.

Pretty simple guidelines must be followed. Allowing for a streak of individuality in every player, these guidelines do not have to be applied rigidly. But it helps to stick to them closely.

Take the grip. The most important thing is that the batsman feels comfortable. And, in most cases, this can be achieved by gripping the bat handle so that the two 'V's between the thumb and forefinger on each hand point down towards the blade. The hands should be as close as possible so that they work together, giving you a better chance of controlling shots. Ideally, the hands should be in the centre of the handle, not choking it near the blade nor allowing it to become too unwieldy by gripping it at the top.

South Australian left-hander, Ken Cunningham, is one of the few successful

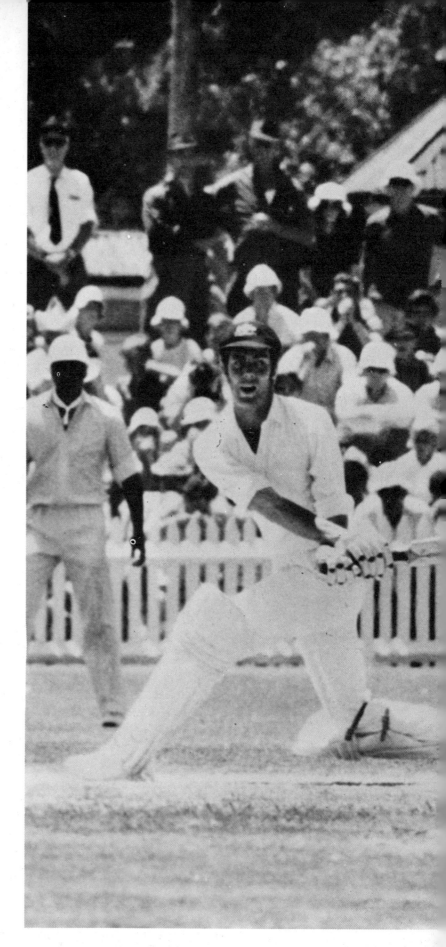

Greg Chappell uses the sweep shot well as he takes four to the boundary behind square leg.

batsmen I know whose hands are apart when he grips the bat. But he does everything else well and has a particularly strong bottom hand.

Cricket is a side-on game, whether you are batting, bowling or fielding. So the stance must be side-on, with your front shoulder pointing towards the bowler.

I prefer to stand with my feet about a bat-width apart and parallel with the crease so that my weight is evenly distributed for ease of movement.

These are a few basic fundamentals and usually the first taught to young players. But too often they are overlooked by too many. A batsman has a much more difficult job to score runs if he makes mistakes with his grip and stance which is why these first principles should be mastered first by young players who are starting off in the game.

When we come to study batting it soon becomes obvious that the basis of this aspect of cricket is defence. No matter how well a batsman plays attacking shots, he still must have the technique to keep out those balls from which he cannot score.

I will come back to some details on defence in a moment, but first of all I want to mention something about backlift which is such an important part of any stroke, whether it be defensive or an attacking shot.

The backlift should be executed as the bowler is about to deliver the ball. The bat should be taken back about stump high to provide that extra momentum to help power and timing in an attacking shot.

Youngsters always are advised to have a straight backlift, even though many first-class players tend to lift the bat towards first or second slip. But it should still come down straight and as close as possible to the front pad.

Coinciding with the backlift, I move slightly back and across, as most batsmen will recommend. It is something of a reflex action in that I want to move slightly before the ball is bowled. I go up on my toes a little, too. I feel comfortable. I haven't really committed myself, and I can still go further back or forward.

It is important not to commit yourself completely too early. Many young players lunge forward and, naturally enough, find it difficult to play back if the ball warrants it.

Greg Chappell is up on his toes to make this shot. The little extra height enables the stroke to be made with more assurance.

In the forward defence, the front foot should be placed as near as possible to the pitch of the ball, and the body weight transferred to the front foot, bringing the head and eyes over the ball so it can be watched on to the bat. The bat, again still as close as possible to the front pad, is angled down, controlled by the top hand and with the elbow bent. The forward defensive shot, as a general rule, is played to a good length ball when you are uncertain whether to go forward or back. The front leg must be bent to allow the weight transference.

Backward defensive shots are played to balls just short of a good length on or outside off stump. The ball normally will bounce waist or chest high, so full use must be made of the space between the creases by moving back *and* across—firstly to cover the stumps and secondly to bring the head and eyes in line with the flight of the ball. The most common fault when playing the backward defence is to move only straight back, leaving the stumps open, and not having the head and eyes in line with the ball.

The weight should be transferred to the back foot. The top hand is still doing the work, the top elbow is bent to angle the bat down, and the bat must be kept close to the body. When the back foot is taken back, the front foot must slide back at the same time to assist balance. It's no good anchoring the front foot.

The forward defence and backward defence are the two most used shots. Once these have been mastered, I would advise youngsters and coaches to concentrate on learning and teaching how to drive forward of the wicket rather than concern themselves with cuts, hooks and pulls. Those shots involve playing with a cross bat and, as a result, there is a greater element of risk.

Apart from the safety angle, straight-bat drives follow on from the forward defence in that the foot movement is much the same. Drives are played to balls which can be reached with one comfortable step forward—not necessarily only to half volleys.

The front foot moves to the pitch of the ball, the weight is transferred to the front foot, and it is most important that the bat follows through in the direction you intend the ball to go. This will help to get full power into the shot. The most common fault is to pull the arms and bat across the body after hitting the ball. This reduces power and increases the risk of mis-hitting or edging the ball.

What particular drive do you play to which ball?

As a general practice, the following should apply:

On drive—ball pitched on middle to leg stumps.

Straight drive—ball pitched on middle to off stumps.

Off drive—ball pitched on or just outside off stump.

Cover and square drives—ball pitched outside off stump.

Don't try to hit the ball too hard. Concentrate on getting the feet into the right position. The top hand still controls the shot. The bat is always straight. The top elbow, bent when contact is made, points, then follows through, in the direction the shot is intended.

If the drives are mastered, there is less need to play what I regard as the risky shots—cuts, hooks and pulls. Certainly they can be used as a variation. But I wouldn't like to depend on them as my main scoring avenues.

Cuts, hooks and pulls are an important part of the game, but they simply don't suit my style like they do, say, Keith Stackpole. 'Stacky' can play them with an apparent lack of risk which suits his style.

I believe my batting has been helped through switching to heavier bats. Ian Chappell's has, too. We believe it assists our timing and ability to play straight.

During the Rest of the World tour of Australia in 1971–72, I was able to have a close look at South Africa's great left-hander, Graeme Pollock. My first impression was how effortlessly he stroked the ball. He didn't seem to use any power at all to get the ball to the boundary. He looked as though he merely leaned on the ball, so precise was his timing.

Pollock used a heavy bat and the lesson I learned from this was that good timing and a heavier bat can help a batsman tremendously. Therefore I decided to try such a bat at the end of the 1972 tour of England. I feel I am now able to concentrate more on the basic fundamentals of batting, knowing that I only have to time the ball for the shot to be worth runs. With a lighter bat, I found I had to do more in the power department, causing mistakes in my footwork.

If a batsman's technique is sound, it should not be necessary for him to adapt to different bowlers to any great degree. The one main exception I make is when facing a left-arm bowler bowling over the wicket or a right-arm bowler bowling around the wicket. Then, I make slight adjustments, angling my feet more towards point, and bringing my left shoulder around more so it still points towards the

bowler. I make sure I am still in the same side-on position I would be in against a right-arm bowler bowling over the wicket.

The biggest obstacle young players must overcome is learning to concentrate for long periods. Concentration goes hand in hand with fitness. If a player is not properly fit, he will find it much harder. Net practice can be used to help concentration. As you bat in the nets, so you probably will play in a match. Concentrate on playing correctly at practice. It should then become more of a habit out in the middle.

Barry Richards, South Africa's magnificent opening batsman, is as near to the perfect batsman I have seen for putting into practice those basic fundamentals—technique, footwork and concentration.

Greg Chappell has put his entire body into this shot and even though he has finished at quite an angle, he has retained his balance.

The photographer just caught the ball in the corner of his picture as it soared from Greg Chappell's bat. The ball kept on soaring until it finally came to rest in the crowd.

The on-side placement stroke

For an on-side placement stroke, generally between mid-on and square leg, Greg makes full use of his crease by moving his right foot back.

Weight is transferred to the right foot while Greg keeps his eyes on the ball and his head down.

Notice the back-lift is slightly across the line of flight, but the bat is straight. This shot is played close to the body, and the left elbow raised high to avoid 'popping' the ball from the top edge.

Max Walker

The art of medium pace and swing bowling

Maxwell Henry Norman Walker has had a meteoric rise to fame. The 190 cm paceman was playing second fiddle in the Victorian side in the December of 1972 and only a few weeks later was Australia's hero.

In the third Test against Pakistan Walker returned the amazing figures of 16 overs, eight maidens, 6–15 to win the match for Australia.

He was selected to tour the West Indies and there established himself as a front-line bowler. Opening the attack in the absence of Dennis Lillee, Walker captured a record 26 Test wickets. After only three Test series, Walker has 54 wickets at an average of 21.

An agile giant, Walker is an excellent field and a useful batsman. Born in Tasmania on 12 September 1948, Walker moved to Victoria in 1967 to play Victorian Football League football with Melbourne and try to develop his cricket.

Fitness is the fast bowler's best friend. Without it he cannot bowl sustained sessions or maintain his pace. What's more, fitness gives a cricketer a better mental outlook on the game, helping him enjoy his cricket.

As a fast bowler I find that running is the best way to get fit, using sprints for acceleration to the wicket and distance runs for stamina.

I know several fast bowlers who train with football teams, and although they don't play in matches, they are able to keep a high level of fitness. Playing football in the winter months has improved my stamina greatly. It is most important to keep fit all the year round. In this way you can move straight into the cricket season rearing to go. This means, of course, a few aches and pains early in the season.

Let me state immediately that I consider myself a fast-medium bowler, not a genuine 'quickie'. There is a great difference between an express fast bowler like Dennis Lillee and a fast-medium bowler like myself. Dennis has

sheer pace on his side. I do not. It is important to evaluate your role in the team's efforts. Generally the genuine fast bowler has the first choice of conditions, taking his pick of ends. This usually means a fast-medium bowler has to bowl into the wind and up the hill. But this should not be a deterrent, because it is part of his role in the team's effort.

The best example I can give of a really good fast-medium bowler is former Australian paceman Alan Connolly. I have been very lucky to have had the chance to play in the same team as Al 'Pal' and see at first hand how he approaches his bowling. He showed repeatedly on the field what a paceman can do without relying on sheer speed. And I might mention here that Al 'Pal' was extremely fit, enabling him to bowl through a complete session, as he had to do on many occasions.

Alan used what I called variables, or in other words, every trick a fast bowler can cultivate. He did it to perfection, eventually becoming Victoria's greatest ever wicket taker.

Basically these variables are: line, length, angle, pace, bounce, swing and cut.

Besides fitness, line and length are the fast-medium's basic weapons. Before a bowler can begin to introduce all these variables into his game, he must have full control of his direction and length. The others will follow. Line and length do not come easily. They are developed through short of hard work in the nets. Once these two basic, but vitally important factors are mastered, the bowler can set out to cultivate a few variations.

Angle is one variable that can be used to advantage. Try using the bowling crease to advantage by varying the angle at which the ball approaches the batsman. Bowl one from wide of the stumps and one close to the stumps.

Another trick of the trade that can stump batsmen is a variety of pace. A batsman can be caught off guard if a slower delivery is slipped in the middle of a fast over.

The amount of bounce in a bowler's delivery can also unsettle the batsman. With a little more concentration in the body action, a bowler can get the ball to rise sharply. It is even worth the bowler's trouble to let the ball go from different heights. Instead of releasing the ball at the top of the arm action, let one go a little later on the down swing. These are some of the tricks that make up a fast-medium bowler's kit.

Another vital aspect of this game must be self confidence. Be confident at all times. You must be confident that you can dismiss a batsman, no matter how great his reputation.

The umpire's finger is raised and the batsman is on his way back to the pavilion. Majid Khan, of Pakistan, is well caught by Marsh off Max Walker.

There's plenty of shoulder in Max Walker's bowling arm, as he shows in this photograph taken while he was practising.

If you don't believe you can do it, more than likely you won't.

Also you must think about the game, and, as a bowler, put yourself in the batsman's shoes. Work out his strengths and weaknesses, hopes and ambitions, and you have gone a fair way to solving the way to get him out.

As I said before, there is no substitute for practice. I like spending at least an hour in the nets, about twenty minutes bowling flat out and another forty minutes working on control of my length and line or maybe trying something new.

I find bowling a fascinating, elusive art, as with any other aspect of the game. You can never stop learning about it. You must have an insatiable desire to learn, but once you think you know it all, that's the end of your progress.

Make a point of learning something new from every game. Talk cricket, watch cricket, and I mean all aspects of cricket. You may think it's funny, but I fancy myself as a batsman. Every bowler should.

There is no reward for going in to bat just for the fun of it. You are there, like any other member of the team, to put runs on the board. And none of this 'save yourself for bowling.' When you are fit, you don't have to save yourself for anything!

Even specialist bowlers should be able to contribute something, so a word on bowling actions. I believe too much is made of bowling techniques, and that many a 'natural' bowling action has been ruined by bowling theory. In search of a new and better bowling action many youngsters struggle to take wickets. Actions are things that should be left to every individual. The acid test is that if you are getting wickets, no matter what your action looks like, keep at it; if you are not getting wickets then you will have to do something to improve your action.

If you have the skill, the variety and the fitness, you can get reasonably satisfying results. Combine all this with the ability to pick a batsman's weakness, his likes and dislikes, get involved in the game and in your role in the team, and you will find cricket far more than just a pleasant form of exercise. It can be an intriguing insurmountable challenge only the fit can hope to conquer.

How NOT to run between wickets. The Pakistanis, Mushtaq (right) and Asif (left) are in the middle of a classic mix-up as they hesitate leaving Max Walker with an easy throw to the bowler's end to complete the run out.

Rodney Marsh

Wicket keeping

The duel between batsman and wicket-keeper. Victorian tailender, Bob Rowan, had his foot in, even if his bat wasn't, as Marsh took off the bails.

Rodney William Marsh was born on 11 November 1947, in West Perth.

A stocky left hander, he is a consistent and powerful wicketkeeper-batsman.

He was dubbed 'iron gloves' after a shaky series against England in 1970–71. Two years later, having taken off weight and worked on his game he was an Australian hero in England.

During the Shield Season of 1972–73 he hammered all attacks and just failed to pass 1000 runs. On this tour he set an Australian record with 23 dismissals.

Any aspiring cricketers who want to be wicket-keepers had better get used to the fact that it is a thankless job. Generally speaking wicket-keepers aren't appreciated by the press, the public or the players. They can't afford to make one mistake; everybody expects them to be perfect.

It's generally accepted that every now and again a catch will go down in other positions on the field. For example, slips fieldsmen are forgiven if a catch is turfed, but wicket-keepers are not.

The 'keeper is virtually the nerve centre of the team. At most times of an innings he will come into the play more than any other player. In top cricket the 'keeper will take anything the batsman misses. Eight times out of ten the 'keeper also will be involved in the play after the batsman has played his shot. The return from the outfield will nearly always come back to his gloves . . . hopefully somewhere close to the stumps.

The aim of a 'keeper is to be perfect. If you don't aim for perfection you will not be tolerated. Half chances behind the stumps must be turned into chances if you're going to be thought of as a top 'keeper. It's these half chances, if accepted, that win matches.

It is hard for me to set down basic rules for aspiring wicket-keepers. To say actually where or how to stand would be silly as these factors are governed entirely by the circumstances. For instance when I'm 'keeping to Dennis Lillee I can look at a wicket, judge its pace and stand where I think the ball will reach me at about waist height. Experience is the only way for young players to learn where to stand when 'keeping to fast bowlers. To say how far apart to keep your feet would also be ridiculous. This is governed by the physique of the player concerned. Naturally if you are a big chap you will have your feet further apart than if you are small.

'Keeping to spin will be the toughest assignment for any keeper. In fact this is what sorts out the wicket-keepers from back-stops. Here, naturally, a 'keeper will stand up to the stumps and crouch. Wicket-keepers crouch, of course, to get a better idea of length and line.

There are three basic essentials for the wicket-keeper: he must have the reflexes of a karate champ, the anticipation of a seven-year-old on Christmas morning and the concentration of a chess master.

Reflexes are usually in-built . . . either you have them or you haven't. If you haven't, then its a waste of time trying to become good.

Anticipation is another of those things that a player develops naturally. A 'keeper must be able to anticipate what a bowler is going to do, what a batsman has in his mind *and* what the fieldsman is going to do!

There is another thing that a good 'keeper will have to pick up fairly quickly. In batting, for example, the great player is the one who can quickly judge the length and line of a delivery. It's the same for the wicket-keeper.

Batting is another facet of the wicket-keeper's job, but it should never be considered his main duty. The main task of a 'keeper is to keep wickets well. If he does that then he has succeeded. Scoring runs is a bonus, and it's only good to get a bonus.

Marsh again, diving full-length to catch West Indian, Clive Lloyd. This is a fine example of the sort of acrobatic action a wicket-keeper needs to be able to perfect.

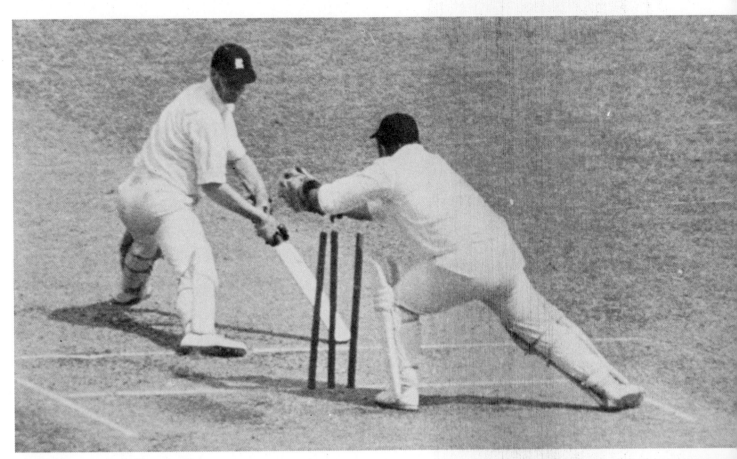

In most sports you'll find that younger players model themselves on a champion. I have looked at all the 'keepers and I think that all the great ones have their own particular style. You can pick up a point here and there, but generally you will develop your own natural style.

In England Alan Knott made a suggestion or two to me, and this is one example of how you can improve your play. But although I now hold my hands in his particular position, I certainly do not resemble Knott in any other way as a wicket-keeper.

Being natural, in fact, is the key-word. One of Australia's truly great wicket-keepers, the late Wally Grout, once said " 'keepers are born, not made."This is true. Most 'keepers, before they start off in their trade, will possess a natural ability for ball games.

I hit a golf ball. Some play squash, others even play football, but they will have this little extra something that will turn them towards cricket and 'keeping.

Completely airborne is wicket-keeper Rod Marsh as he stretches to take this extra-ordinary catch from a firmly-hit leg glance which seemed to be safely turned.

Down to earth this time, Marsh had to dive low instead of high but he still picked up the catch.

I did not set out to be a 'keeper. Like most other kids I wanted to be an Alan Davidson or a Richie Benaud. Taking wickets and making runs was to me far more glamorous than standing up in pads and hot sweaty gloves taking the balls that the batsmen missed.

But I was lucky; the coach of the school team thought I might make it as a 'keeper. That was the start. Once I got a few stumpings and took a few catches I was determined to become a wicket-keeper.

Though cricket teams all have captains, more often than not it's the wicket-keeper who will set the tone and enthusiasm of the fielding. He is the boss. Of course the captain will tell everybody what to do, but the players will in most cases look to the 'keeper for example.

Take care of them and they will take care of you. I have even noticed that after I have taken a catch the bowler concerned will try that much harder with his fielding. The returns to the 'keeper seem to improve. I don't know quite what it is, but they do seem to put more effort and concern into their work on the field.

I can readily recall that there was a big panic on before I played my first Test Match for Australia. The generally accepted 'keeper for that series against England was Brian Taber and my selection in front of him may have taken a few of the pundits by surprise.

The thing that seemed to worry most people was the fact that I hadn't had any experience 'keeping to John Gleeson who, at that stage, was considered to be one of the main barbs in the Australian attack.

The first Test of that series was played in Brisbane and I must admit I was a little nervous about it. I saw out the 'quicks' without too many problems, then came the big test . . . Gleeson was brought into the attack. Early in his first spell of bowling he did not have much success with his leg-breaks and 'wrong uns'.

Then he bowled an orthodox off-spinner halfway down the track. Geoff Boycott took a good look at it and then got ready to help himself to another four. He slashed at the ball, it took the edge, and a split second later the ball was in my gloves and I was jumping up and down, appealing.

Boycott got a shock; I got a shock, and Gleeson got his first wicket of the series. And there it was: Boycott c. Marsh b. Gleeson. The wicket was Gleeson's, but at least I hadn't muffed it. Even though I hadn't 'kept to him before in top cricket I had to learn fast and adjust.

If you don't adapt quickly you won't be around long enough to worry about it!

The backward defensive stroke

Greg Chappell shows clearly here the first essential of a good backward defensive stroke—a straight back-lift.

With head and eyes over the ball, Greg begins to 'pack up', getting his complete body behind the ball. His bat comes straight forward.

The high left elbow again ensures
a straight bat as Greg watches the
ball onto the bat. Bat and pad are
close together to give the ball no
chance of passing.

Kerry O'Keeffe

Leg spin bowling

Kerry James O'Keeffe, born 15 November 1949, is a talented right-arm leg-spinner who has yet to fully mature. He made his debut in first class cricket against Queensland in 1968–9. O'Keeffe played only four Test matches before being selected to tour the West Indies in 1973. But he did not lack experience. He played for English county club Somerset in 1971 and 1972, taking 96 wickets and scoring 865 runs. A useful right-hand batsman, he has scored more than 2000 runs

Australia's cause looked lost that day at the Queen's Park Oval, Port of Spain in Trinidad.

It was the luncheon break on the final day of the Third Test between Australia and the West Indies, and our players sat moodily in the dressing-room apprehensive that, after two draws, the West Indies were poised to break through.

They needed sixty odd runs with seven wickets in hand.

Some Australian players stretched out, exhausted by the torrid morning session, others just sat on the benches, their arms covering their faces.

But the astonishing resilience of Ian Chappell's 1973 team was demonstrated with the very first ball after lunch. Alvin Kallicharan, who had played magnificently on a pitch tending to bounce and spin inconsistently, flashed at a Max Walker out-swinger and edged it into Rodney Marsh's safe gloves behind the stumps.

This was the glimmer of hope we needed. Fieldsmen and bowlers lifted themselves to a supreme effort and wickets fell regularly.

We were one wicket away from victory when Keith Boyce flashed at one of my leg-spinners which turned sharply, caught the edge and Ian Chappell, at slip, flung himself high to his left

to take an extraordinary catch. Australia had won against all odds and we went on to take the Fourth Test and the series two-nil.

I felt a tremendous sense of achievement both because Australia had won and because I had played a big part by capturing my Test-career-best of four for 57. My performance had proven to me three things.

First, I realised I could succeed at Test level. Secondly, I saw the importance of accuracy when conditions are offering more than customary assistance. Thirdly, it became clear that when bowling to left-handers (the West Indies had four of them—Fredericks, Lloyd, Kallicharan and Willett) the line of off-stump and outside it was of paramount importance.

Early in the West Indies' second innings at Trinidad I had erred by bowling on the legs of the left-handers who swept and hooked consistently. Only when my confidence grew did I concentrate solely on bowling line and length and allowing the responsive wicket to do the rest. This illustrates the importance of basics at all levels of cricket.

I am sure it is the ambition of every young cricketer to play for his country. For a leg-spinner I can vouch that it is a long hard road. For every successful day there will be many frustrating, less fruitful days. Just how the leg-spinner emerges from those trying days, just how he reacts to heavy punishment, will decide how far he progresses along cricket's path to top honours.

The basic grip to bowl the leg-spinner—from which the 'googly' or 'wrong un' also is bowled—is to hold the ball so that it settles into the first three fingers. The first two fingers lie across the seam with the top joints taking most of the pressure. The third and little fingers are curled below them so that the top joint of the third finger, lying along the seam, presses hard upward against it. The third finger is the main lever for the spin. The wrist is cocked and brought over at delivery while the third finger propels the ball forward in an anti-clockwise direction.

The googly or wrong'un is bowled with the same grip. However, the wrist turns over earlier and is bent back so that at release the back of the hand faces the batsman and the ball comes out from over the top of the third and little finger spinning in a clockwise direction.

A great catch. Kerry O'Keeffe dismisses Rohan Kanhai off his own bowling with a splendid lunge across the pitch.

Kerry O'Keeffe balances himself at the point of delivery as he bowls at the nets during a practice session.

Field Placement

Leg-spinner to a right-hander on a good, hard wicket

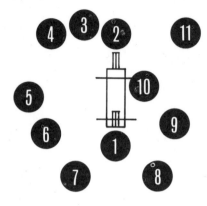

1. Bowler	7. Mid-off
2. Wicket-keeper	8. Mid-on
3. First slip	9. Mid-wicket
4. Short backward point	10. Forward short leg
5. Cover-point	11. Short backward square leg
6. Extra-cover	

This is an attacking field where the batsman has to wrest the initiative from the bowler. The square leg can be pushed back to the fence if he begins to sweep to break up the field. All fieldsmen are saving the single.

Leg-spinner to a left-hander on a fast, good wicket

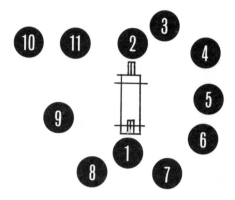

1. Bowler	7. Mid-off
2. Wicket-keeper	8. Mid-on
3. First slip	9. Mid-wicket
4. Short backward point	10. Backward square leg
5. Cover	11. Short backward square leg
6. Extra-cover	

This field is set to contain the left-hander. If he is in trouble bring number 10 up for catching at short leg.

Leg-spinner to a right-hander on a slow, turning wicket

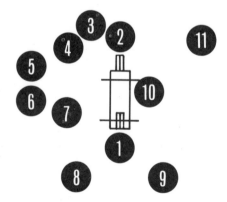

1. Bowler	7. Short extra cover
2. Wicket-keeper	8. Mid-off
3. First slip	9. Mid-on
4. Second slip or gully	10. Short forward leg
5. Short forward point	11. Short backward square leg
6. Cover	

This is an attacking field with a responsive wicket. When the wicket turns it is advisable to bring in a second slip or gully for the thick outside edge. If your wrong'un is pitching, you may need two men close-catching on the leg side. All men are saving the single.

Leg-spinner to a left-hander on a slow, turning wicket

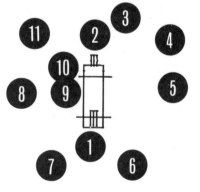

1. Bowler	7. Mid-on
2. Wicket-keeper	8. Mid-wicket
3. First slip	9. Short forward leg
4. Short backward point	10. Short leg
5. Cover	11. Short backward square leg.
6. Mid-off	

Two men are close catching on the leg side. Number 8 maybe moved and put at second slip. All men are saving the single.

The young leg-spinner, once he has mastered the orthodox grip, must then work out for himself an easy run-up leading into the basic action for a leg-breaker, which requires a side-on delivery, bowling across the body and with a follow-through braced against the left foot.

The arm should be as high as possible to enable maximum bounce to be obtained.

In first-class cricket, a spinner who bounces a great deal can be more awkward to handle than one who spins a great deal. Richie Benaud was a great example of a champion leg-spinner who possessed bounce. Bobby Simpson, a masterful player against leg-spin, once said he found it more difficult to play the sharply bouncing ball than a sharply turning ball.

At the point of delivery, the left arm should be high and the back foot parallel to the bowling crease. The ball is delivered across the body, bracing on the left foot and following through across it.

My advice to aspiring leg-spinners is first to become proficient at length and direction. Afterwards, the variations can be exploited. It is a fundamental mistake to attempt too much variation if you cannot control your stock delivery ball. This control can only be developed through persistent net practice and the leg-spinner should practise in the nets as though he were bowling in a match.

If you are alone at the nets, mark a spot on a good length and endeavour to pitch on that spot with every delivery. When running into bowl, whether in a match or at practice, keep your eyes firmly placed on the spot where you intend pitching the ball.

Richie Benaud had such a perfectly balanced run-up and delivery that he was able to bowl to me in a net with his eyes shut, yet pitch his deliveries on a length so perfect that the ball spun past my bat. That was the result of constant practice, co-ordination of run-up, delivery and follow-through.

Variations such as change of pace—that is, bowling slower or quicker—are performed this way: the slower ball is allowed to leave the hand slightly before the normal delivery point, the quicker ball slightly after the normal delivery.

On the subject of length, a leg-spinner will find the ideal length is a pitching spot to a batsman were he can neither play it easily on the half-volley (overpitched) or play it easily off the back foot (too short). The bowler will quickly perceive if he is bowling too full or too short by the manner in which a batsman finds freedom to counter his deliveries.

You should remember that tall players have extra reach so that they can get down the pitch to drive or smother spin more easily than shorter players. Therefore, the leg-spinner must quickly 'read' the strength and weakness of a new batsman and bowl to a plan to counter strong points and to exploit faults in technique or attitude such as being too casual or too aggressive.

If a batsman is driving consistently, though he is not getting to the pitch of the ball, slow a delivery with no perceptible change in action. Allow the ball to leave the hand slightly before the normal delivery point. A catch in the covers or mid-off may result.

In analysing a batsman's weakness, I must stress that the leg-spinner must operate to a plan. There must be a different tactic employed against each batsman.

For example, if a bowler sees that the batsman does not 'read' the wrong'un, he should not make the mistake of bowling it every second ball but should try to work the batsman into a position where he is least expecting it. Bowl him an over of leg-spinners, then first ball of the next over, another wrong'un. He may play for the leg-spinner and be bowled by the ball coming back the other way and which comes between bat and pad. It is surprising how few players are constantly on the watch for slight variations.

The most important part of leg-spin bowling is trajectory, and the leg-spinner must work out for himself the pace that suits his stock delivery. I have found that I am more effective by beating the batsman off the pitch than by flight. By bowling slightly quicker than the average leg-spinner I am able to 'hurry off' the harder wickets enabling me to earn L.B.W. decisions and clean-bowled.

To summarise then, my advice to all young leg-spinners is first to develop a balanced run-up and delivery; to practise remaining side-on for as long as possible at delivery; to practise following through against the braced left foot; and, most importantly, to concentrate on the spot where you plan to land the delivery.

To all leg-tweakers—keep practising. It is the only ingredient for success in our art. The rewards are great if the effort is forthcoming.

Ross Edwards

Practise, concentrate and keep fit

Ross Edwards was born on 1 December 1942 in Cottesloe, Western Australia. He is a hard hitting middle-order batsman and one of the world's best cover fields.

At 29 Edwards was considered by many as 'too old' to tour England in 1972. However, with a string of centuries behind him he won selection in England and posted his highest first class score : 170 not out as an opener in a Test.

Cricket is what Everest must have been to Sir Edmund . . . the supreme challenge. Hillary, of course, achieved his goal, but overcoming the challenge of cricket is, in its own way, more difficult. The more elusive a goal is, or the harder the challenge, the more satisfying are the rewards. But cricket is really unconquerable, so any small measure of success is extremely satisfying.

A batsman's task is to succeed in the scoring of runs. In trying desperately to do so he will encounter a few arch enemies along the way. He usually has a fleet of good bowlers to contend with, an opposing captain using all his guile plotting against him, eleven fieldsmen on their toes waiting anxiously for that mistimed shot and a piece of turf that will sometimes play some nasty tricks.

Success is not always measured purely on the number of runs scored. By this I mean that most of the good players I've talked to don't regard their best innings as the one in which they have scored their highest numbers of runs, but the one in which they have succeeded in the most difficult circumstances.

I consider my two best innings as those played in a Sheffield Shield game against South Australia in Adelaide in the 1971–72 season. The pitch for that match was a spin bowler's paradise, with the ball jumping at different heights and turning all over the place.

Even in good batting conditions the wily Ashley Mallett is a handful for any batsman and during this match he reached the nightmare category. It was in fact a full time job just to stay in. Each innings I batted for about two hours, scoring 40 in the first innings and 20 in the second, and during all that time I can remember Mallett bowling only one bad ball. It was in fact that ball that I got out to in the second innings. It was because of the extremely difficult conditions that I regard these two innings as my best.

Although cricket has its satisfactions, rewards and disappointments, it is, after all, a game, and, above anything else, should be enjoyed. If it ever becomes drudgery, then you are playing the wrong sport.

Take practice. In top cricket, long and sometimes arduous hours must be spent in practice. These, too, must be enjoyable and can be made so by striving always for improvement. It is important to practice as hard (or, if possible, harder) as you would play in a match. I believe in batting as hard in the nets as I do out in the centre during a game, with absolute concentration and application.

Another player who adopts this attitude with his cricket is Western Australian John Inverarity. At the nets he is a model subject. He will treat each ball as though he's in the nineties grafting for another century. As a player Inverarity also makes the most of everything he has got, and this is another lesson for every young cricketer.

All batsmen have capabilities. Some can hook, some can drive, some can cut—but few players can play all the shots. What you have to learn is to bat within your capabilities.

If a player realises he has a weakness, this aspect should be practised over and over again until the weakness no longer exists. In net practice it may be hard to get enough of 'that' ball which is giving concern, but this doesn't mean that it stops there and that you wait for the next practice session in a couple of days to try and sort it out.

It should be sorted out straight away. Team spirit comes into the game here. Providing you're a team player ready to assist others who require some help, then you shouldn't have any trouble organising somebody to help you. What you need is someone to throw one ball after another at you, at the spot where you're having

A fine action shot by Ross Edwards. Note how he is balanced on his toes with his body angled forward to get as much power as possible into the shot.

70

the difficulty, until playing that particular shot becomes second nature. When the same ball appears in a game you will find that you will play the shot correctly, automatically.

As a batsman you must occupy the crease, or, in other words, don't get out, stay in. You can't get runs sitting in the pavilion.

There's a bit of 'ringcraft' attached to successful batting. By not playing shots until you are ready you can make bowlers bowl where you wish. If you are concentrating hard enough, they will make mistakes before you do.

One of the important things about batting is confidence. If you don't feel confident about playing a shot, the solution is simple: don't play it.

Defence—that's the key. Develop a tight, well-organised defence and you'll always take some shifting. The thing about it is that if you can stay in long enough, and wait for the bad balls, the runs will come.

Another important thing to remember is not to play 'get-out' shots. Being over-confident and chasing that ball outside the off stump leads to many a downfall. Tighten up, be patient and then all of a sudden the ball will be bowled in the place where you want it and you'll start to play your shots and build your innings.

At times, of course, you'll run into some tight bowling. You'll be pinned down, frustrated by field placings and even the slow hand-clapping of the crowd might start to get to you. This is a red alert for a batsman. It is important at this point not to lose your nerve. Don't panic. Concentrate on staying there, and these periods of play will pass and runs will start to flow again.

Another important facet of a batsman's make-up is his running between the wickets. A player can easily get lazy in this department and cost his side, as well as himself, runs. It's not a bad idea to call every ball until you get used to running with your partner. There are only three calls: 'yes', 'no' and 'wait'. That sounds very simple, but it's surprising how often the process is bungled by experienced players, resulting in a lost wicket.

Fitness is one of the most important factors governing the success or failure rate of any sportsman. If you are fit, you can last it out and you will win through in the long run. Endurance is very important in cricket. When you become tired, mistakes follow and this is what you are trying to avoid. Fitness applies to all departments of cricket. Become lazy and sloppy and your game will be affected.

Fielding, though a team matter, is also a very personal thing. Adopt the approach that it is you against the batsman. Don't let him get any runs if you can help it, and again enjoy the long hours in the field. The better fieldsman you can make yourself, the more pleasure you will have in the game. Fielding is certainly one department where a player can improve himself out of all sight.

These days I field in the covers more than anywhere else. I take pride in my fielding, but it can be said that I started my career as a wicket-keeper. In fact it was as a 'keeper that I got my first game with the Western Australian side.

To be successful and to enjoy cricket it is necessary to be determined, have a tough attitude and work hard. The best cricketers have these qualities. Take Geoff Boycott; he's a really tough competitor who relishes beating the bowlers into subjection. The Australian captain, Ian Chappell, is another fine example of this. A different sort of dedication can be seen in Keith Stackpole, who played much of his early first-class cricket as a middle-order batsman and spin bowler. He doesn't bowl much now, but his batting has improved to the extent that he could open the batting for Australia with distinction. 'Stacky's' effort in England during the 1972 tour was a wonderful example of just what application will achieve for a cricketer.

Not everyone has the abilities of these players, but if you have just average ability you can make it.

When I started playing cricket I was fully aware of my limitations, but I worked hard and, though I haven't conquered the game, I have had some measure of success, and that's what it's all about. That is the enjoyment of cricket.

Even at the nets Ross Edwards is a model of concentration as he plays this defensive shot.

'keeping

This delivery was a leg-break, moving to Rod's right. So he transferred his weight back to his right foot as he kept behind the ball.

Gloves are now firmly placed together, allowing the ball no space to pass. Rod, remaining in a semi-crouched position to get a better view of the movement of the ball, has his eyes fixed on it as it is about to reach him.

It is important not to 'snatch' at the ball. Rod shows how the ball comes comfortably into his gloves.

Lou Rowan

The main laws of the game

Lou Rowan was one of Australia's most outstanding umpires. He umpired 75 first-class matches, 26 of them Tests, and also three internationals between Australia and a World XI. Rowan formed a remarkable partnership with Col Egar; they stood in a record 19 Tests together.

Rowan, a 183 cm black-haired father of eight, is a detective-sergeant by occupation. He was involved in many controversial incidents during his umpiring career, including the Ian Meckiff throwing affair, the Ray Illingworth walk-off and the John Snow incidents at Sydney.

Young cricketers do not welcome an invitation to study the laws of cricket with much enthusiasm. Yet those who take the trouble to study the laws can give themselves a greater all round knowledge of the game, which makes them better equipped to play it.

While many lessons can be learnt on the field of play from mistakes and missed opportunities, a knowledge of the laws of the game is necessary for a player to gain the most from his cricket. Too often a young player is unable to take advantage of an opportunity simply because he is unaware of the options that are open to him. Besides, many incidents which happen on the field could have been avoided if the players concerned had been familiar with the laws.

At the present time there are 47 laws, all of which are vital to the proper conduct of the game. Some of these may seem to have little relevance but they are there for a purpose. From time to time legislators change or vary the laws for what they consider to be valid reasons. Not all of the changes are good, but nevertheless they are made, and players must become familiar with them.

Young players do not always have the advantage of first class umpires. In the case of the 'player umpire' as frequently happens, the fieldsman is asking a question of an umpire whose knowledge may be slight. Now if the player is not sure of the law, and the player-umpire is also in doubt, how can the game function as was intended? The way to avoid the possibility of 'incidents' and unpleasantness is to know the laws.

Small boys quickly learn simple points such as the number of players permitted in each side; the number of balls to the over; the length of the pitch; the number of stumps; boundaries, and so on. In the main, the laws the young cricketer should concentrate on are those connected with conduct on the field of play: the rights of the batting side and the fielding side; the matter of legitimate deliveries and attempts to score runs. He should know his own entitlements.

Possibly one of the most important laws is Law 25 which deals with 'Dead Ball'. The law provides that the ball comes into play as the bowler starts his run to the bowling crease, or commences his bowling action. From that point onwards the ball remains in play until such time as a boundary is scored, a wicket falls, or the ball has finally settled in the hands of the bowler or the wicket-keeper. The ball should not be regarded as 'dead' while there is some chance of the fielding side gaining an advantage. In most cases the ball is 'dead' when it is obvious that both sides believe that ball is no longer in play. If batsmen respect the rights of the fielding side, they will not be caught in some unguarded moment. The batsman, if he is in any doubt, should check with the umpire, and once the umpire has decreed the ball to be 'dead' no danger exists to the batsman.

Law 26 is one law that has caused an enormous amount of trouble. It deals with the delivery of the ball to the batsman, and covers such matters as 'suspect bowling', and 'no-balling'. A number of books and countless articles have been written on the former, and I believe that the worst thing a player can do is to become a suspect bowler. He will be surrounded by controversy and will not gain the pleasure and satisfaction that he should expect from the game. Any bowler who, for one reason or another, becomes suspect, should do all in his power to rectify the problem, and never be afraid to go to those who will give him an honest answer as to whether or not his bowling action is suspect. He must be prepared for the truth. The main

It's a no ball and Rod Marsh takes the opportunity to swing hard.

thing to avoid is the sudden straightening of the bowling arm in the delivery action. It is as simple as that.

Another section of Law 26 deals with the position of the bowler's feet. The bowler's back foot must not touch the return crease or its forward extension when he is bowling, and although he is now permitted to have his front foot on the popping crease, he must not put his foot over the line in delivering the ball. Some part of the front foot, whether grounded or raised, must be behind or on the line.

Quite a number of bowlers prefer to bowl from behind the popping crease, as this removes all possibility of being 'called' on the position of the front foot. The bowler is entitled to have the front foot on or over the return crease and its forward extension. It should be remembered that the ball does not become 'dead' on the call of 'no ball'. For those interested, there are four ways of being dismissed from a 'no ball': run out; hitting the ball twice; obstructing the field; handling the ball.

'Wides' are a relatively simple matter. The point to consider here is that if the ball is too high or too wide for the batsman to reach when standing in a normal position, the call of 'wide' should be made. The batsman can negate what might otherwise be a 'wide' by covering the ball. Anyone foolish enough to be dismissed from a 'wide' should not only not mention the matter to anyone, he should retire from the game!

Leg byes are in order if the deflection of the ball from any part of the striker's person has, in the opinion of the umpire, been unintentional. If the umpire is of the opinion that the deflection was not unintentional, he calls 'dead ball' as soon as one run has been made. The batsmen return to the ends from which they came. The wicket is 'down' once the bails or a bail has been completely removed from the top of the stumps. A mere disturbance of the bails is not enough. If the bail does lodge between the stumps after being removed from the top, the wicket is held to be 'down'. That type of miracle incident is not common.

Law 33 provides that a batsman may retire at any time, but may not resume his innings without the consent of the opposing captain, and then only on the fall of a wicket. I doubt if anyone would claim that the best interests of this great game would be served if a captain were to refuse a batsman the right to refuse an innings. Much would depend on the circumstances but young players should be slow to refuse on points like this.

In the case of the striker being 'caught', it

should be remembered that the ball must have made contact with the bat, or the hand holding the bat, but not the wrist. Of course the ball must not be allowed to touch the ground. The fieldsman must have both feet within the playing area at the instant the catch is completed. The matter of boundaries is therefore extremely important. Commonsense and good sportsmanship will help to overcome a lot of difficult situations. There are times when only the fieldsman knows whether or not he has 'made' the catch. Sporting gestures by players in the doubtful cases are to be encouraged.

Some confusion exists on the matter of 'hitting the ball twice'. Players have nothing to worry about, providing the second hitting of the ball is not with the intent to score runs. The batsman would be in trouble if he manifests his intent to score by some act, such as moving down the pitch as in running between the wickets. But unless there is some act which indicates the batsman was attempting to score from that second strike, nothing should eventuate. The only time runs can be scored from the second striking of the ball is when overthrows result.

The batsman is out 'hit wicket' if he hits down his wicket with his bat or with any part of his person—and this includes his clothing and equipment—at any time when playing at the ball, or when setting off for his first run immediately after playing at the ball. For the purposes of this law it matters not whether the batsman was attempting to hit the ball or whether he was attempting to avoid the delivery.

Law 39, which deals with 'leg before wicket', is one of the most difficult laws in the minds of most young players, and indeed, some senior players too. It is safe to say that all batsmen, at some time or other, are victims of bad decisions under this law. Young players should study it closely, and in doing this, they will have no difficulty in realising that every effort has been made over the years to clarify the law. It now reads as follows:

The striker is out 'leg before wicket' if with any part of his person except his hand, which is in a straight line between wicket and wicket, even though the point of impact be above the level of the bails, he intercepts a ball which has not first touched his bat or hand, and which, in the opinion of the umpire, shall have, or would have, pitched on a straight line from the bowler's wicket to the striker's wicket, or shall have pitched on the off side of the striker's wicket, provided

always that the ball would have hit the wicket.

Notes:

1. The word 'hand' used in this law should be interpreted as the hand holding the bat.

2. A batsman is only 'Out' under this Law if *all* the four following questions are answered in the affirmative.
   (i) Would the ball have hit the wicket?
   (ii) Did the ball pitch on a straight line between wicket and wicket (and this case includes a ball intercepted full pitch by the striker), or did it pitch on the off side of the striker's wicket?
   (iii) Was it part of the striker's person other than the hand which first intercepted the ball?
   (iv) Was that of the striker's person in a straight line between wicket and wicket at the moment of impact, irrespective of the height of the point of impact?

It should therefore be kept in mind that presuming all other requirements are met, there are only two situations in which the ruling should be 'not out'. The first is when the ball is pitched outside the line of the leg stump; the second is when the ball is outside the off stump, and the batsman has made a genuine attempt to play the ball with the bat. It is true that players add to the problems by making some quite unnecessary appeals, and umpires

Lou Rowan has a glass of champagne to celebrate his retirement. Joining him are Ian Chappell, Peter Pollock and Gary Sobers.

must concentrate at all times to avoid being caught unawares.

There is little to worry about in the matter of obstructing the field. Quite frequently the obstruction is unintentional and therefore not 'wilful' as required by the law.

The requirements of the law relating to 'run out' are quite simple. Great care should be exercised to ensure that the right batsman is given 'out' when there is something of a mix-up. Once the batsmen have passed in running, he that is running to the wicket that is broken, pays the price.

It is the umpire who must remain continually alert to handle appeals for 'stumping'. In most cases the question is a simple matter of the order in which the events occur. If the batsman has not regained his ground, the decision is easy.

Of all the laws to be studied and understood the most important for the proper conduct of the game is Law 46. This law is a long, and in some respects, involved one. It sets out the duties of the umpires in ensuring that the conduct of the game and the implements used are strictly in accordance with the laws. It makes clear that the umpires are the sole judges of fair and unfair play; the fitness of the ground; weather, light and so on. This law sets out just what the fielding side may do as regards polishing the ball. It deals also with the matter of bowlers running on the pitch;

bouncers; time wasting, and gives the umpires the power to ensure the proper conduct of the game. All players should make a detailed study of this law so that they will know the procedure to follow as regards appeals against conditions, etc.

Finally I would like to point out that although it is accepted that all umpires do sometimes make mistakes, it should be appreciated that the first mistake is made by the players. If there were no errors of judgement on the part of the players, the umpire would not be called upon to adjudicate. But this is all part of the game. I would, however, urge that all young players bear in mind that when people who have been involved in the playing of the game at all levels offer advice, it is not to inflict their views upon the youngsters, but to point out to them some of the pitfalls which are a fact of life. I urge players to not insult the game by misconduct of any type, on or off the field. No amount of talking or any quantity of words will erase the damage done.

Regardless of your feelings, never stand and argue with umpires. Not only is this an offence under Law 46, it is an affront to the game. Hasten slowly in any move to gain an advantage through the employment of skills and tactics likely to bring about some form of rebuke from officials on or off the field of play.

Cricket is the all time great sport. Play it hard, play it tough, but play it fair. It is a testing time for the young and an opportunity for the moulding of character. Remember that it is a game and not a war, and while many pleasures are to be had from the proper playing of games, there are no pleasures from the wars.

Umpire Rowan appears unperturbed as England captain, Ray Illingworth, and fast bowler, John Snow, argue with him just before the famous 'walk-off' at the Sydney Cricket Ground during the last MCC tour of Australia.

Richie Benaud

Teaching cricket

Richie Benaud sends one down
during a practice session at the
Melbourne Cricket Ground before
a big match.

Richie Benaud is a former great all-rounder and captain who spearheaded Australia's cricket revival at the start of the sixties. He holds the record for the greatest number of wickets taken by an Australian player—248.

Benaud was considered one of the world's most outstanding leg-spinners and was also a useful batsman, scoring 2201 runs in Tests. He captained Australia in 27 Tests, winning 12 and losing only four. He was the Australian captain in Test cricket's only tie, against the West Indies at Brisbane in 1960–61.

Enjoy your cricket! That is the first and most important advice that can possibly be given to any youngster desiring to play the game at a level ranging from the smallest junior club 300 kilometres from a city to the teenager who aspires to wear the green and gold cap of Australia. Talking at length on one occasion with Sir Donald Bradman, he produced for me a phrase which will forever remain in the mind: 'If the game is not enjoyed, then why bother to play it at all.' Why indeed? No matter what one does in this modern age, enjoyment should come first providing no harm is done to other members of a team and certainly one eye should always be kept on providing entertainment and enjoyment for the spectator who pays his money at the gate.

There are many methods of becoming a cricketer and I stress here that I have no intention of talking of becoming a great cricketer, but merely of one who sets out to play the game, derive full pleasure from it and then, if possible, improve to the extent of moving up the ladder into a higher sphere of cricket.

I began learning about the game somewhere between the ages of three and six in a country town in New South Wales. The town was

Jugiong, and I used to go and watch my father play on Saturday afternoons. He was an extremely good country cricketer who later became a very good city player, taking over 600 First Grade wickets with the Central Cumberland Club in Sydney.

In those early days though, if I wanted a game of cricket during the day, it had to be by playing my own Test matches in a concrete walled room attached to the school house and this was really the manner in which I started off learning how to play the game. These days however facilities are so much improved that the youngster, even at an early age, has the benefit of coaching and age group cricket teams that will soon sort out whether or not he has initial ability.

Personally I believe much young talent has been missed over the years in Australia because of lack of coaching of the correct kind, though I do not advocate massed group coaching, which is inclined to turn out robot-like cricketers.

The system in Australian cricket, in general terms, is divided into junior cricket, senior cricket, first-class cricket and then, as the ultimate, Test matches against other countries. In the past it was something of a rarity for country cricketers to eventually make the Test side and the matter would be commented on with some awe by overseas people who would remark how strange it was that a young player could come up from such a background to wear the green and gold cap. Now, it is difficult for a young cricketer of talent to avoid the eagle eye of the Test selectors in each capital city and there are many country players of quality who make their mark on the first-class scene.

There are many old-time cricket followers in Australia who speak with pride of the fact that Australian cricketers in the top bracket have never been coached—'they are all natural players' is the cry. That, to me, is either wishful thinking or sheer nonsense—take your pick! In some way, every cricketer of any stature has been coached; either by others, or by his own adherence to the basic fundamentals of the game. There are other aspects such as temperament, ability to play well under pressure and quick thinking which add to the natural ability of the really good players but, with rare exceptions, they are all close followers of the fundamentals of batting and bowling and, generally speaking, they have all been good fieldsmen.

Many people will tell you that players like Bradman, O'Reilly and Compton, three greats of the game, were unorthodox and never followed the coaching book. However, a close study of their batting and bowling actions at the crucial moments immediately shows they have the basic fundamentals of the game so well organised that the opposition have less chance against them than against any ordinary player. Sir Donald Bradman, for example, although regarded as an unorthodox batsman, when shown on the slow motion screen is superb in defence; so too is Denis Compton. That great Australian bowler, Bill O'Reilly, may have looked awkwardly menacing, but, stop him at the instant of delivery, and you will see one of the finest basic fundamental bowling actions imaginable.

There is no substitute for hard practice and then, after that is finished, another session at the nets. Tie that in with adherence to the basic fundamentals and you have immediately arrived at a situation where a boy has a real chance of progressing in the game. I have already mentioned how I used to play my own Test matches against a wall, with the ball bouncing back and the strokes then played to various parts of the room. A number of variations of that type of cricket will immediately come to the mind of the reader although these days most of the practice and coaching is done in the nets on a concrete pitch.

Let's take each department of the game in turn. Most people look at batting as the most important and enjoyable part of the game because it involves the attacking of the bowler and the consequent exercise on the part of the fieldsman in chasing the ball. To get down to basics, the young cricketer should arrive at his batting grip by placing the bat on the ground, with the handle facing him, and then picking it up with both hands together, round about the middle of the handle.

It is most important that he doesn't start off with a ridiculously unorthodox grip and that is the reason for suggesting this method—it is very difficult to pick up the bat from the ground with both hands with anything but a good grip. You try it some time and you will see exactly what I mean. A reasonable guide is that the 'V' formed by the thumb and first finger of the left hand would point to the left shoulder as the batsman takes his stance, and the 'V' formed by the thumb and first finger of the right hand would point to the right shoulder in the stance. This applies, of course, to a right-hand batsman.

As in golf, the grip has a tremendous bearing on what then happens in the swing and it is quite important that a youngster starting off in the game should be set up with the correct grip. Most boys will consider that not only do they have the correct grip but, before the coach gets anywhere near them, they also have sorted out their stance and the way they should play their strokes. But again it is necessary carefully to watch the basic fundamentals to ensure that the stance is comfortable and not exaggerated, that the feet are the same distance on either side of the batting crease, and that if a line were drawn from the middle stump to the crease then the toes of both feet should be on that line.

Possibly the most important thing in preparing yourself for the instant when the bowler is about to deliver the ball is to make sure that your eyes are level; that the level of your right eye (in the case of a right-hander) is

John Benaud, younger brother of
Richie, swung hard at this ball but his
timing wasn't right and it went through
to the keeper.

The fundamentals of batting

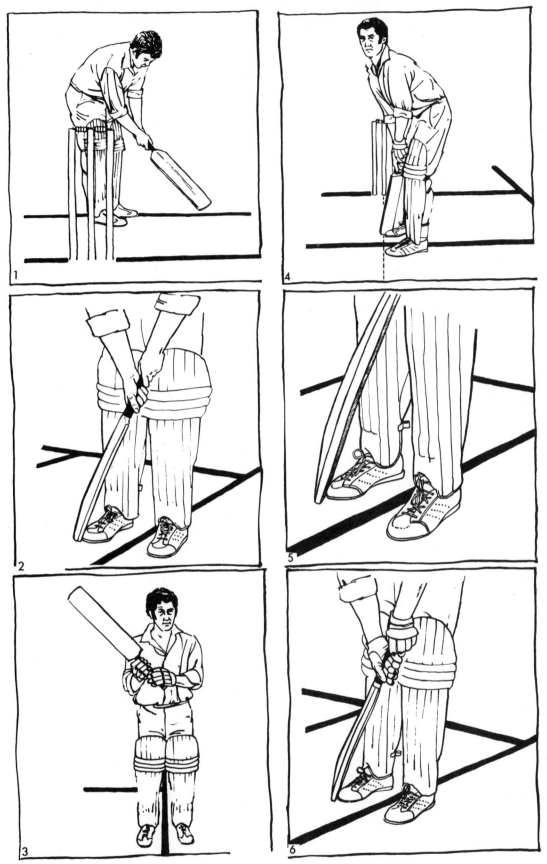

1. The batsman picks up the bat with both hands, making sure that his hands are close together.

2. The feet are at equal distance either side of the batting crease. Again, the hands are together and the bat is positioned behind the right toe.

3. Another angle of the feet, at equal distance either side of the batting crease.

4. The eyes are level. The toes are in a line drawn from middle stump to middle stump.

5. The bat is behind the right toe.

6. The left hand rests gently on the top of the left pad, with the back of the left hand pointing towards extra cover.

The forward defensive stroke

INCORRECT
Bat is away from body

Ball can get through gap

Incorrect
Bat is away from body
Ball can get through gap

The front foot is placed as near as possible to the pitch of the ball and the stroke begins.

CORRECT
Bat close to pad

No gap left

Correct
Bat close to pad
No gap left

The backward defensive stroke

Correct
Body well behind ball and bat close to pad
No gap left

An excellent forward defensive position with head right over the ball, foot to the correct line, and the bottom of the bat well behind the handle, so as to avoid giving a catch to the close-in fieldsmen.

Even at this angle it can be judged that there is no gap between bat and pad, and that the left elbow is well up without being exaggerated.

Incorrect
Bat is well away from body allowing the ball plenty of room to get through.

OFF-DRIVE

STRAIGHT DRIVE

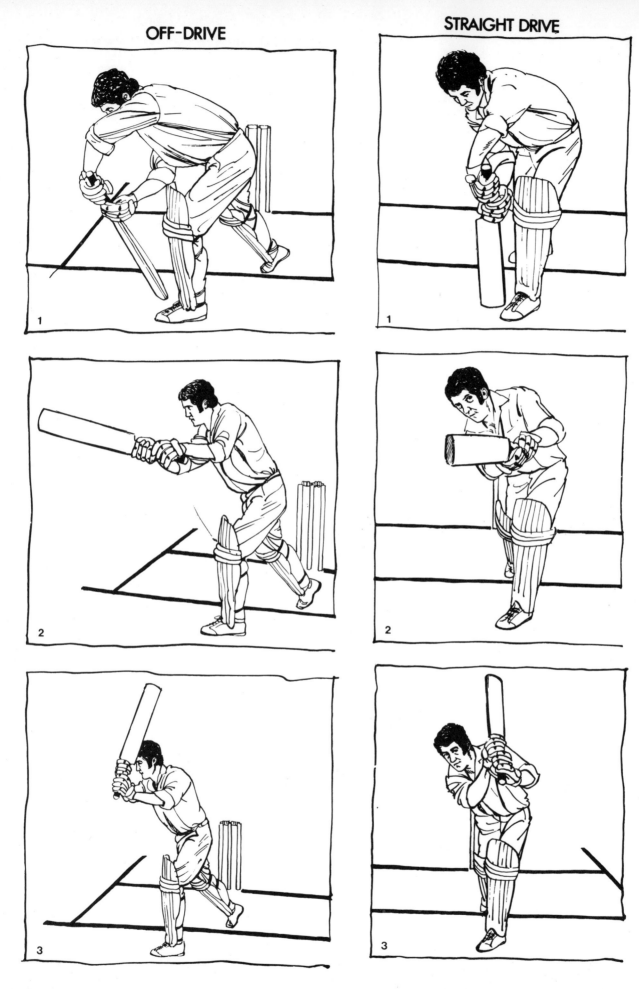

The off-drive

1. Foot to the ball.
2. The shot is made and the follow-through begins.
3. The follow-through is completed with the weight on the front foot.

The straight drive

1. The straight drive is similar to the forward defence.
2. Foot and body are further round facing the bowler.
3. The follow-through is completed perfectly.

The on-drive

1. Foot to the ball. Bat beside the pad.
2. The shot is made and the follow-through begins.
3. The follow-through is completed with the weight on the front foot.

ON-DRIVE

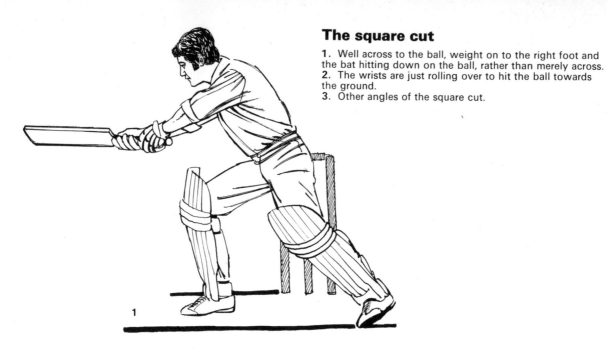

The square cut

1. Well across to the ball, weight on to the right foot and the bat hitting down on the ball, rather than merely across.
2. The wrists are just rolling over to hit the ball towards the ground.
3. Other angles of the square cut.

SQUARE-CUT

BACK-CUT

The back cut

Across to the ball with the foot closer to the stumps than the square cut. Wait until the ball is past the body but in line with the back foot before making the shot.

THE PULL

THE HOOK

The pull shot

1. It is important for the body to be behind the line.
2. The wrist is rolled over the ball so that it is played towards the ground.

The hook shot

1. Unlike the pull shot, the hook is played with the batsman inside the line.
2. The bat is in the air behind square-leg.
3. The wrists are rolled over.

not below the level of your left. Even at Test match level, I have often found myself falling into this bad habit of leaning away to the offside and, if a Test match player can do it, then you can imagine how easy it is for a youngster on the way up.

The final point in the initial fundamentals of batting is that the top of the left hand should rest on the front pad; this is done to avoid pushing the bat handle out towards point.

The first thought of any young batsman should be that, when the bowler runs in, he will hit the ball (not slog it) to the boundary. That can be done either through a vicious cover-drive or an elegant back cut or glance. But his first thought should be in attacking vein. Then he runs down the scale, scoring as many runs as possible if a boundary proves to be impossible—three for a straight drive, two for a stroke off the pads, one for a quick single. In the event of the bowler having been too good for him, he plays the ball defensively. Some coaches teach the opposite; that the defensive stroke should be thought of initially and then that should be turned into an attacking blow. But I have always believed in my way—otherwise the game would become purely one of defence and the bowler would be allowed to get on top.

When going to schools to coach, I am always astonished to see that the basic fundamentals of the game are so wantonly neglected. Send me to a school with 200 young cricketers and I will find you 195 who have not been shown the basic fundamentals of batting and, worse still, are most unlikely ever to become good bowlers because of their method of bowling front-on rather than keeping side-on in delivery. I always knew when I had turned front-on in bowling because the ball landed short and the batsman usually hit it out of the park or up against the pickets. It was just one of those things you could sense at the instant of delivery and it is for this reason I am so adamant that there is only one way to start off a young bowler and that is with the side-on fundamentals. Occasionally you will find front-on bowlers who, because of sheer strength and extraordinary natural ability, will make it to the top but, believe me, they are a rarity.

Any young bowler reading this should get one of his friends to watch him in the nets next time he bowls and make sure of the following points:

His back foot lands parallel with the bowling crease.
His left arm is pointing up to the sky as his right arm starts to come over for delivery. He is looking over his left shoulder and inside his left arm.
Finally, and most important, his eyes have never left the spot on the pitch where the ball is to land.

A good example is to stand and do those things, i.e. put your right foot down parallel and six inches behind an imaginary bowling crease; extend your left foot so that it would land where the batting crease would be; put up your left arm and look over your left shoulder at the spot on the pitch where you want the ball to land. I will bet in ninety-nine cases out of one hundred that is not the bowling action you are using at the moment—but it is the one you should use in the future.

It is not possible in a Chapter of this kind to go deeply into the technicalities and guile of bowling but, for any young player interested in improving his bowling, the two vital words are *line* and *length*. By line I mean that you should select a spot on the pitch at which to aim so that when the ball hits it, if unimpeded by the batsman, it would hit middle and off stump or, at the worst, middle stump. Again this applies to right-hand bowlers over the wicket to right-hand batsmen. The reason for choosing this line is that even if you bowl close to the stumps there will be a natural slanting angle that would take the ball outside leg stump if bowled any further across the pitch.

The aim always should be to bowl out the batsman but, at the same time, that should not be taken to mean that accuracy can be sacrificed on the off-chance of getting a wicket. To line add the word length; that means the ball should land on such a spot that it is not quite possible for the batsman to drive off the front foot, nor is it quite possible for him to force you away off the back foot. Your line makes it impossible for the batsman to square cut or hook you and therefore you will have bowled a ball good enough for the batsman to be unable to score.

The fundamentals of bowling

1. The back foot is parallel to the bowling crease.
2. The left arm is reaching for the sky and the eyes are looking over the left shoulder and inside the arm.
3. Another view of the bowler about to deliver, still with the back foot parallel and still looking over the left shoulder.
4. The delivery should be started from about face level. The arm is about to describe a complete circle.
5. Bowling action is complete and the right arm has come across the body—in fact the bowler is bowling in front of his front leg.
6. Another angle of the follow-through.

The off-spin grip

1. The ball is held firmly, with the index finger the main one used in imparting spin.
2. It is important that the back of the hand faces to mid-wicket (in the case of a right-hand bowler) when the ball is delivered.

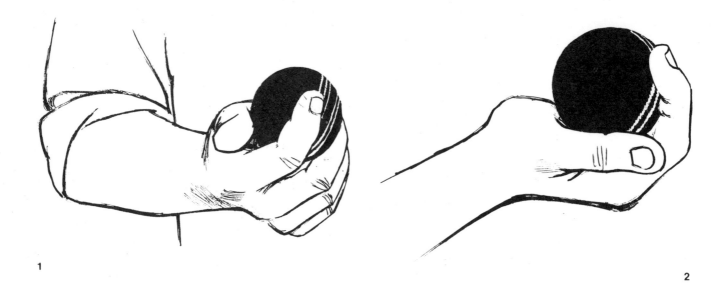

1

2

The inswinger grip

1. The seam points to fine-leg.
2. The inswinger from another angle.
Seam to fine-leg.
Batsman.

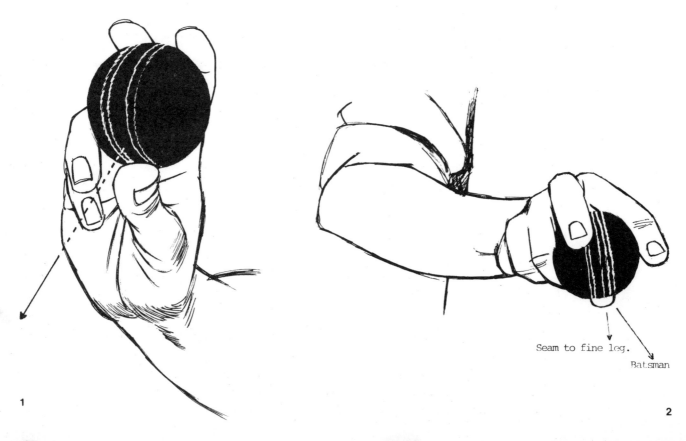

Seam to fine leg.

Batsman

1

2

Grip for the leg-break, overspinner, skidding topspinner and wrong 'un

The hand is just about to turn so that when the ball is delivered, the back of the hand will be to the bowler's face.

The back of the hand faces the on-side in the instant before the wristwork begins.

The first knuckle of index finger and first knuckle of third finger are on the seam of the ball.

The thumb is used merely as a balancing agent.

The ball must be SPUN, NOT ROLLED.

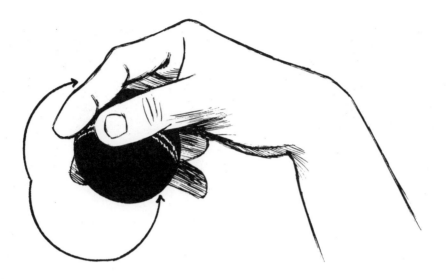

The outswinger grip

1. The fingers are in an orthodox position with the index and second finger either side of the seam.

2. The seam is pointing from the bowler's hand towards the first slip. Note that the thumb is on the seam underneath the ball. If the thumb is allowed to be at the side of the ball the bowler will tend to spin the ball rather than keep the seam upright. This rule applies to the inswing as well as the outswing.

A variation of the outswinger

3. The outswinger from another angle.
Batsman.
Seam to first slip.

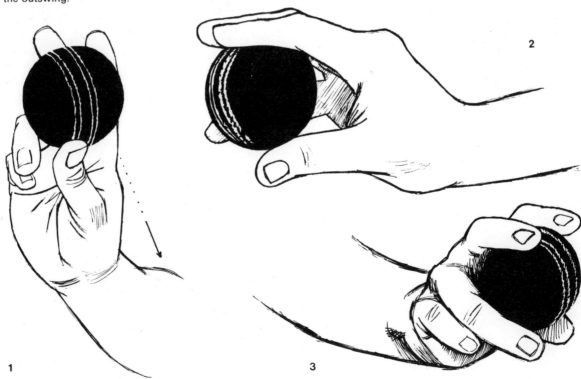

The leg-cutter grip

A medium-pace bowler able to bowl a leg-cutter poses many problems for the batsman. In fact, this ball is a fast leg-break, and the bottom illustration shows much the same grip as for the leg-break.

However, the cutter comes very much out of the fingers rather than with the degree of wrist work of the leg-break. The grip is shown from two angles
The work is done with the second finger

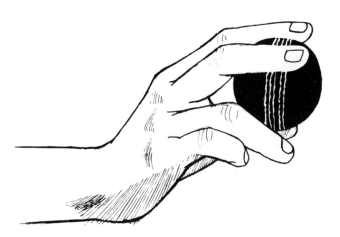

Richie Benaud in his bowling days lets one go at the nets. Benaud was one of Australia's greatest leg-spin bowlers.

That is the basic fundamental of bowling—that you should have the correct action. And by that I mean very definitely the correct orthodox action and, to that, you should ally line and length. That is the prime requirement for every bowler who ever picks up a ball to *attack* a batsman. Notice that the thought of defending against a batsman never comes into it and, if you are a fast bowler, medium pacer or slow bowler, your aim should always be to attack and take wickets. You should never allow yourself to become completely mechanical, otherwise the batsman will be quick to seize on this and give you a fearful pasting.

I remember one day in Sydney in 1959 when I apparently got into the habit of dropping my shoulder every time I bowled a 'wrong un' and, in the course of the afternoon, Peter May hit me to most parts of the ground. A quick check with wicket-keeper, Doug Ford, at the end of the day showed us what was wrong and the following day I bowled 24 'wrong uns' in succession to May with a high arm action, eventually getting him out.

It is always wise to vary your bowling as much as possible and not just make the art into a chore of mechanically bringing over your arm. A bowler should at all times know what his tactics are going to be against any batsman, particularly if he has ever bowled against him at an earlier date. He must have a retentive memory and be able to recall the batsman's weakness—even though he may have eradicated that weakness since the last time you saw him. Then you just have to devise new tactics and devise them very quickly.

So too with the captain who must have split second timing with his decisions and be aware of the strengths and weaknesses of every player in the opposition team—*and in his own side*. The reason for the emphasis on the latter phrase is that most captains at a youthful level don't bother about the weaknesses of their friends but only their strengths, and it is most necessary to know about, say, a left-arm bowler who hates bowling to left-handers or a fast bowler who can bowl only four overs at a time.

A tactical appreciation of captaincy is, to my way of thinking, based largely on good fortune and, to a lesser extent, on skill. I am not trying to say that skill does not provide a necessary starting point and, in fact, it is rare for anyone to become a captain without possessing the various qualities required to lead a team. But cricket is so much a game of luck that some of the best captains can finish up with the worst records and, although the reverse does not apply to the same extent, it can happen that a captain can be extremely unlucky over a short period of time.

To lose the toss, for example, in a Test series where three of the five Tests are played on spinning pitches, is sheer bad luck rather than lack of skill, and there is not a great deal a captain can do about it. I would suggest to any budding captain that at all times he keeps in his mind the word attack and that, wherever possible, he does just that. Even when it is necessary to defend, and there are plenty of occasions, a young captain should never be negative in his approach to a defensive situation.

Negative leg side bowling provides no enjoyment for anyone, certainly not the people watching at the ground, and again the word enjoyment should come into every captain's vocabulary. Generally speaking, the orthodox field placings for different types of bowling can be recommended, but it is always as well for the young captain to look at the opportunity of removing a man from a defensive position—say, third man or fine leg—and putting him in a catching position—say, slip or leg slip. The more wickets taken the more chance of winning the game, and then the more enjoyment for everyone on the captain's side.

There are no special qualities needed to play cricket; perhaps there are some special qualities needed to reach the top. But all these are outweighed, in my view, by the word practice. Hour after hour, day after day, the young batsman or bowler should practice until he is as close to perfect as one could ever be in what is basically a game of chance. But, above all, remember that this is a game to be enjoyed and a game to be played in ethical fashion. The user of sharp practice and the 'shrewdy' will have their day but it will be over a short-lived period, and the one who really enjoys his cricket is the one who stays with the ethics of the game.

In the modern era the controversial is newsworthy and much is often made of matters to do with players and umpires. Let me finish with just one stricture for all young cricketers and that is that the umpire's decision should always be not only respected but obeyed. Far too often when there is an appeal the players involved do not look towards the umpire and pay him the respect of acknowledging his presence. Cricket is a game of character and of character-building and this is one area where every cricketer should play his part. Obey the umpire's decision and help him as much as you can, as well as helping your team and your team-mates—but, above all, enjoy your cricket.

The fundamentals of wicket-keeping

1. The weight is evenly balanced on the balls of both feet.
2. The feet are approximately 46 cm apart. Relax and crouch comfortably.
3. Fingers point down, up or sideways—never at the ball.

4. Concentrate on every delivery because each one is a potential wicket.
5. Be fully aware of your position in relation to the stumps.
6. Never snatch—always let your hands give with the ball. Rise with the ball.

The fundamentals of fielding

1. The eyes are on the ball and the fingers are pointed down towards the ground for a close-to-wicket catch.
2. Again, the fingers point down, rather than at, the ball.
3. The body is behind the ball.
4. The ball is being watched right into the hands.
5. In throwing, the right foot is positioned at right angles to the target.
6. Weight is just about to go on the front foot, as the ball is about to be thrown.

The forward defence stroke

Greg Chappell shows the basic principles in playing forward defence. He keeps a straight back-lift and places his left foot in line with the direction of the delivery.

Greg keeps his eyes directly in line with the ball and his bat comes through along the line of the delivery. Notice Greg's right hand is loose on the bat handle. This gives his guiding left hand full control, and will help him keep the bat on a defensive angle.

He holds his left elbow high to ensure a perfectly straight bat.

The broad face of the bat greets the ball. Greg still has his left elbow high.

Throughout Greg kept his head down and his eyes on the ball. He left no space between bat and pads.

The follow through shows Greg with his head still down and his eyes still on the ball. Greg's excellent balance is shown by his right foot—it never left the ground behind the crease.

Ian Redpath

The fundamentals — gear and grip, block and stance — and playing slow bowling

Ian Richie Redpath, with 52 Tests to his credit, is Australia's most experienced player. A delicate right-hand batsman, especially against slow bowling, he is a consistent run-maker.

Redpath was a surprise omission from the 1972 touring team to England, but fought his way back into the Australian team with 240 runs at an average of 48 in the three tests against Pakistan in 1972–73.

Formerly an opening batsman, Redpath dropped down the batting order with success in the early seventies, but was recalled to the opening berth against Pakistan. He was a success against the West Indies when giving Australia a sound start in each Test.

Redpath is a handy medium-pace bowler who does not bowl for Australia, and is a snappy close in-field. He was born in Victoria on 11 May 1941.

Cricket is a confidence game. When you are confident the runs flow, but a lack of confidence generally means a lean spell. Confidence is an untouchable quantity. One day you have it, the next day it has gone. If you are determined enough, you will always get it back—sooner or later.

But often it is the little incidentals that can give a player confidence. Things small, but vital, such as gear, batting stance and grip— and a stern look at your technique.

Let's look at gear. I have always maintained that if a person is to play the game seriously, he must firstly acquire the correct equipment.

The matter of dress is important and, I feel, reveals just how keen a player is about the game. Whether you have creams, whites, boots or sandshoes, you must always have them clean when you take the field.

First, it puts you in the right frame of mind. And, equally important, it can be a confidence booster if the whole team walks out looking clean, keen and business-like. This approach to being well-dressed should not stop at playing a match. It should be pursued at practice.

You can't be wearing clean gear every training night, but at least dress for cricket. Don't turn up looking as though you are heading for the beach, or for a burst of football training. Keeping your boots up to scratch is another necessary factor in cricket. We all tend to wear them in a match and be content not to cast our eyes on them until the next match. But that simply won't do. You must constantly check your boots. There has been many a run-out or missed catch at a vital stage of a game because of a loose or missing sprig.

Batsmen should have their own essential equipment. Then they don't have to rely on what is in the team kit.

You must have a good pair of padded batting gloves and, just as important, a thigh pad to wear under your creams. Because cricket is such a confidence game, you have to have everything going for you from the start. Many bad habits can form if you don't wear a thigh pad. Too often I see a player lacking the confidence to get behind the ball on the leg side. This is often caused by some painful blow on the unprotected leg at some time in a player's career.

That instrument which always seems too narrow—the bat—is also very important. Not for obvious reasons like hitting the ball, but because the wrong type of bat can hold a player back.

Never use a bat that is too heavy for you, especially if you are still young and growing. Using a bat that is not suited to your build can cramp your style and be your downfall in many innings. If you don't have your own bat and must use one from the kit, use the same one all the time. It's important to have a bat you like and can use confidently.

Stance and grip are two other factors that can give a batsman confidence. When you walk to the crease you must feel comfortable in both. If you don't you cannot have confidence in what you hope to achieve.

Let's take stance first. Most first-class players have their feet parallel and about a foot apart. This enables them to push off with either foot when playing forward or back.

Once again Ian Redpath has used his feet swiftly and well to come some way down the wicket to loft a slow spinner well over the bowler's head.

I don't believe in having the feet placed together as this tends to cause a batsman to over-balance when moving. The knees should be slightly bent and the front shoulder pointing either straight down the wicket or between mid-on and the bowler.

It should not be turned any further around towards the square-leg umpire as this restricts off-side shots in front of the wicket. You then find you have trouble in moving your front foot and head across to deliveries on or outside the off stump. In this era when bowlers concentrate on bowling on or about the off stump, it is essential that the batsman is sound in that area.

Grips depend largely on the type of player you are, but let me suggest a grip that allows you to play shots on both sides of the wicket.

The top hand (left hand to a right-hand batsman): If you draw a line from the outside edge of the bat upwards, it should pass through the knuckle at the base of the index finger.

The bottom hand: The 'V' formed by the thumb and index finger should be turned slightly towards the outside edge of the bat.

The top hand should always be held firmly to lift the bat on the backlift, while the bottom hand supplies the power for the shots. This helps to keep the backlift straight and the elbow well up. If you lift the bat with the bottom hand it will inevitably go towards point and result in a cross-bat shot.

Once the fundamentals are known, it is then up to the individual's talent and practice to do the rest.

I find one of the most fascinating battles in cricket is playing spin bowling.

Stance, and the ability to be able to move equally well with either foot, is a crucial part of playing spin. You have to be able to move quickly to smother a good delivery, and be fast enough to hit any loose ball that comes along.

There are two ways to counter a spinner, one is to anchor yourself to the crease and wait for the loose one. If you are not fast on your feet this method could be considered the safest.

I don't like that style because it gives the bowler a chance to dictate the terms, and the higher you go in cricket the fewer are the loose balls that come along. I prefer to move down the pitch and take the initiative.

By moving quickly, either down the wicket or well back onto the stumps, a batsman can force a bowler to change his routine. His normal good length delivery is either over-pitched or short, so he is usually forced to adopt an unaccustomed variation, often resulting in the loss of accuracy and more scoring opportunities for the batsman.

The best way to counter the off-spinner is to keep playing off the front foot. In this way you are ready to drive the over-pitched ball and also ready to smother the good length delivery with forward defence.

But in playing forward you must keep your bat and pad close together to prevent the ball from finding the gap between them and taking your stumps.

A word of advice on pitches and off-spinners. If the ball is spinning a lot don't try to cut or you run a grave risk of being caught behind the wicket as the ball comes in sharply towards the stumps and cramps your style.

If it is short enough to hit off the back foot, stroke the ball through covers rather than take the risk of a cut. Two of the best exponents of this style are Greg Chappell and Keith Stackpole. Neither leaves the crease but both have such good judgement that they find it easy to attack or defend.

Greg always plays strongly in front of the wicket either off the front or back foot and never cuts against the spin. 'Stackie' is a good example of sweeping with the spin on the leg-side deliveries, and strongly crunching the ball through the covers off the back foot to off-side deliveries.

If 'Stackie' is well set, he will give the bowler something to think about by hitting hard and high over the close-in fieldsmen. He simply keeps his head down, waiting for the right ball.

Leg-spinners are countered in a similar fashion to an 'offie', except that the ball leaves the right-hander instead of turning into him. Because of this you should try to play slightly outside the line of flight when playing defensively to avoid an edge.

Leg-spinners rely heavily on variations of flight, so it is essential to get right to the pitch of the ball whether defending or driving. You must also go well back if forced on to the back foot.

Many young players find spinners rather overwhelming. They get confused, frustrated and disheartened. Practice in the nets against spinners is the only remedy. Practise until you can play them confidently.

You can't avoid them, so you should try to conquer them. All it takes is practice, and that key word, *confidence*.

A stylish shot from Doug Walters as he off-drives. His front foot is well forward, his back foot is still in the crease and the bat is straight.

Down the wicket goes Ian Redpath,
one of the best players of slow bowling
in the Australian team. He uses his feet
swiftly to get to the pitch of the ball and
places it through the field.

Laws of the Game

(1947 Code—4th Edition)

OFFICIAL

London
Marylebone Cricket Club
1968

World Copyright Reserved

Preface

During the last two hundred years the conduct of the game of Cricket has been governed by a series of Codes of Laws. These Codes were established as indicated below, and were at all times subject to additions and alterations ordained by the governing authorities of the time. Since its formation in 1787 the Marylebone Cricket Club has been recognised as the sole authority for drawing up the Code and for all subsequent alterations.

There is little doubt that Cricket was subject to recognised rules as early as 1700, though the earliest known Code is that drawn up in 1744 by certain Noblemen and Gentlemen who used the Artillery Ground in London. These Laws were revised in 1755 by 'Several Cricket-Clubs, particularly that of the Star and Garter in Pall-Mall.'

The next arrangement was produced by 'a Committee of Noblemen and Gentlemen of Kent, Hampshire, Surrey, Sussex, Middlesex and London,' at the Star and Garter on 25 February 1774, and this in turn was revised by a similar body in February, 1786.

On 30 May 1788, the first M.C.C. Code was adopted, and remained in force until 19 May 1835, when a new Code of Laws was approved by the Committee. The Laws appear to have been first numbered in 1823.

The 1835 Code, amended in detail from time to time, stood until 21 April 1884, when, after consultation with cricket clubs both at home and overseas, important alterations were incorporated in a new version adopted at a Special General Meeting of the M.C.C.

By 1939, these Laws supplemented as they had been by the inclusion of many definitions and interpretations in the form of notes, were in need of revision, and immediately on the conclusion of the World War the opinions of controlling Bodies and Clubs throughout the world were sought, with the result that the present code was adopted at a Special General Meeting of the M.C.C. on 7 May 1947.

This revision in the main aimed at the clarification and better arrangement of the previous Laws and their interpretations, but did not exclude certain definite alterations designed firstly to provide greater latitude in the conduct of the game as required by the widely differing conditions in which it is played, and secondly to eliminate certain umpiring difficulties.

This, the fourth edition of the 1947 Code, contains a few small alterations to the Laws and certain alterations and amendments to the Notes published since 1962.

Under the Rules of the Marylebone Cricket Club the Laws of Cricket can only be changed by the vote of two-thirds of the members present and voting at a Special General Meeting, of which due notice is required to be given.

From time to time the Committee of the M.C.C. are required to give interpretations on points of difficulty arising from the Laws, and these are given in the form of notes to the Laws themselves.

The primary purpose of the book as expressed by the late Sir Francis Lacey (Secretary of the M.C.C. from 1898 to 1926) remains unchanged:—

'The aim of this publication is to remove difficulties, which are known to exist, although they are not always apparent. Hundreds of cases are sent to the M.C.C. for decision every year. It is from this source that the chief difficulties have become manifest. Saturday and League Matches are especially productive of disputes, and it is hoped that those who read these notes may find an answer to any doubt which may arise as to the proper interpretation of the Laws of Cricket.'

Lord's Cricket Ground,
London, N.W.8.
1st June, 1968.

S. C. GRIFFITH,
Secretary, M.C.C.

The term 'Special Regulations' referred to in certain Laws are those authorised by M.C.C., Overseas Governing Bodies or other Cricket Authorities in respect of matches played under their jurisdiction.

(A) The Players, Umpires and Scorers

1 A match is played between two sides of eleven players each, unless otherwise agreed. Each side shall play under a Captain who before the toss for innings shall nominate his players who may not, thereafter be changed without the consent of the opposing Captain.

Notes

1 If a captain is not available at any time, a deputy must act for him to deal promptly with points arising from this and other Laws.

2 No match in which more than eleven players a side take part can be regarded as First-class, and in any case no side should field with more than eleven players.

Substitutes

2 Substitutes shall be allowed to field or run between the wickets for any player who may during the match be incapacitated from illness or injury, but not for any other reason without the consent of the opposing Captain; no Substitute shall be allowed to bat or to bowl. Consent as to the person to act as substitute in the field shall be obtained from the opposing Captain, who may indicate positions in which the Substitute shall not field.

Notes

1 A player may bat, bowl or field even though a substitute has acted for him previously.

2 An injured batsman may be 'Out' should his runner infringe Laws 36, 40, or 41. As *Striker* he remains himself subject to the Laws; should he be out of his ground for any purpose he may be 'Out' under Laws 41 and 42 at the wicket-keeper's end, irrespective of the position of the other batsman or the substitute when the wicket is put down. When *not the Striker* the injured batsman is out of the game and stands where he does not interfere with the play.

The Appointment of Umpires

3 Before the toss for innings two Umpires shall be appointed one for each end to control the game as required by the Laws with absolute impartiality. No Umpire shall be changed during a match without the consent of both Captains.

Note

1 The umpires should report themselves to the executive of the ground 30 minutes before the start of each day's play.

The Scorers

4 All runs scored shall be recorded by Scorers appointed for the purpose; the Scorers shall accept and acknowledge all instructions and signals given to them by the Umpires.

Note

1 The umpires should wait until a signal has been answered by a scorer before allowing the game to proceed. Mutual consultation between the scorers and the umpires to clear up doubtful points is at all times permissible.

(B) The Implements of the Game, and the Ground

The Ball

5 The Ball shall weigh not less than $5\frac{1}{2}$ oz (155.9 grams) nor more than $5\frac{3}{4}$ oz (163.0 gram). It shall measure not less than $8\frac{13}{16}$ in (22.4 cm). nor more than 9 in (22.9 cm) in circumference. Subject to agreement to the contrary either Captain may demand a new ball at the start of each innings. In the event of a ball being lost or becoming unfit for play, the Umpires shall allow another ball to be taken into use. They shall inform the Batsmen whenever a ball is to be changed.

A small ball, weighing $4\frac{3}{4}$ oz (134.7 gram) should be used by young boys. The Women's Cricket Association standard ball weighs 5 oz (141.8 gram) and is slightly smaller than the standard size.

Notes

1 All cricket balls used in First-class matches should be approved before the start of a match by the umpires and captains.

2 In First-class matches, the Captain of the fielding side may demand a new ball after the prescribed number of overs has been bowled with the old one. The Governing Body for cricket in the country concerned, shall decide the number of overs applicable in that country, which shall be not less than 75 overs, nor more than 85 overs (55 to 65 eight ball overs).

In other grades of cricket, these regulations will not apply unless agreed before the toss for innings.

3 Any ball substituted for one lost or becoming unfit for play should have had similar wear or use as that of the one discarded.

The Bat

6 The Bat shall not exceed $4\frac{1}{4}$ in (10.8 cm) in the widest part; it shall not be more than 38 in (96.5 cm) in length.

The Pitch

7 The Pitch is deemed to be the area of ground between the bowling creases, 5 ft (1.52 m) in width on either side of the line joining the centre of the wickets. Before the toss for innings, the executive of the ground shall be responsible for the selection and preparation of the Pitch; thereafter the Umpires shall control its use and maintenance. The Pitch shall not be changed during a match unless it becomes unfit for play, and then only with the consent of both Captains.

The Wickets

8 The Wickets shall be pitched opposite and parallel to each other at a distance of 22 yd (20.12 m) from stump to stump. Each Wicket shall be 9 in (22.9 cm) in width and consist of three stumps with two bails upon the top. The stumps shall be of equal and or sufficient size to prevent the ball from passing through, with their top 28 in (71.1 cm) above the ground. The bails shall be each 4⅜ in (11.1 cm) in length, and, when in position on the top of the stumps, shall not project more than ½ in (1.3 cm) above them.

Notes

1 Except for the bail grooves the tops of the stumps shall be dome-shaped.

2 In a high wind the captains may agree, with the approval of the umpires, to dispense with the use of bails (*See* Law 31, Note 3).

The Bowling and Popping Creases

9 The Bowling crease shall be in line with the stumps; 8 ft 8 in (2.64 m) in length with the stumps in the centre. The popping crease shall be marked 4 ft (1.22 m) in front of and parallel with the bowling crease and shall extend a minimum of 6 ft (1.83 m) either side of the line of the stumps. The return crease shall be marked at each end of the bowling crease, at right angles to it, and shall extend forward to join the popping crease, and a minimum of 4 ft (1.22 m) behind the wicket. Both the return and popping creases shall be deemed unlimited in length.

Note

1 The distance of the Popping crease from the wicket is measured from a line running through the centre of the stumps to the inside edge of the crease.

(C) The Care and Maintenance of the Pitch

Rolling, Mowing and Watering

10 Unless permitted by 'Special Regulations,' the Pitch shall not be rolled during a match except before the start of each innings and of each day's play, when, if the Captain of the batting side so elect, it may be swept and rolled for not more than 7 minutes. In a match of less than three days' duration, the pitch shall not be mown during the match unless 'Special Regulations' so provide. In a match of three or more days' duration, the pitch shall be mown under the supervision of the Umpires before play begins on alternate days after the start of a match, but should the pitch not be so mown on any day on account of play not taking place, it shall be mown on the first day on which the match is resumed and thereafter on alternate days. (For the purpose of this Law a rest day counts as a day). Under no circumstances shall the Pitch be watered during a match.

Notes

1 The umpires are responsible that any rolling permitted by this Law and carried out at the request of the captain of the batting side, is in accordance with the regulations laid down and that it is completed so as to allow play to start at the stipulated time.

The normal rolling before the start of each day's play shall take place not earlier than half an hour before the start of play, but the captain of the batting side may delay such rolling until 10 minutes before the start of play should he so desire.

2 The time allowed for rolling shall be taken out of the normal playing time if a captain declare an innings closed either, (*a*) before play starts on any day so late that the other captain is prevented from exercising his option in regard to rolling under this Law, or (*b*) during the luncheon interval later than 15 minutes after the start of such interval.

3 Except in the United Kingdom, if at any time a rain affected pitch is damaged by play thereon, it shall be swept and rolled for a period of not more than ten consecutive minutes at any time between the close of play on the day on which it was damaged and the next resumption of play, provided that:—

(i) The umpires shall instruct the groundsman to sweep and roll the pitch only after they have agreed that damage caused to it as a result of play after rain has fallen warrants such rolling additional to that provided for in Law 10.

(ii) Such rolling shall in all cases be done under the personal supervision of both umpires and shall take place at such time and with such roller as the groundsman shall consider best calculated to repair the damage to the pitch.

(iii) Not more than one such additional rolling shall be permitted as a result of rain on any particular day.

(iv) The rolling provided for in Law 10, to take place before the start of play shall not be permitted on any day on which the rolling herein provided for takes place within two hours of the time appointed for commencement of play on that day.

Covering the Pitch

11 The Pitch shall not be completely covered during a match unless 'Special Regulations' so provide; covers used to protect the bowlers' run up shall not extend to a greater distance than 3½ ft (107.7 cm), (1.07 m) in front of the Popping creases.

Note

1 It is usual under this Law to protect the bowlers' run up, before and during a match, both at night and, when necessary, during the day. The covers should be removed early each morning, if fine.

Maintenance of the Pitch

12 The Batsman may beat the Pitch with his bat, and Players may secure their footholds by the use of sawdust, provided Law 46 be not thereby contravened. In wet weather the Umpires shall see that the holes made by the Bowlers and Batsmen are cleaned out and dried whenever necessary to facilitate play.

(D) The Conduct of the Game

Innings

13 Each side has two innings, taken alternately, except the case provided for in Law 14. The choice of innings shall be decided by tossing on the field of play.

Notes

1 The captains should toss for innings not later than 15 minutes before the time agreed upon for play to start. The winner of the toss may not alter his decision to bat or field once it has been notified to the opposing captain.

2 This Law also governs a One-day match in which play continues after the completion of the first innings of both sides (*See also* Law 22).

Following Innings

14 The side which bats first and leads by 150 runs in a match of three days or more, by 100 runs in a two-day match, or by 75 runs in a one-day match, shall have the option of requiring the other side to follow their innings.

Declarations

15 The Captain of the batting side may declare an innings closed at any time during a match irrespective of its duration.

Notes

1 A captain may forfeit his second innings. In this event, the interval between innings shall be 10 minutes and his decision must be notified to the opposing captain and umpires in sufficient time to allow seven minutes rolling of the pitch.

16 When the start of play is delayed by weather Law 14 shall apply in accordance with the number of days' play remaining from the actual start of the match.

Start and Close of Play and Intervals

17 The Umpires shall allow such intervals as have been agreed upon for meals, 10 minutes between each innings and not more than 2 minutes for each fresh batsman to come in. At the start of each innings and of each day's play and at the end of any interval the Umpire at the Bowler's end shall call 'Play', when the side refusing to play shall lose the match. After 'Play' has been called no trial ball shall be allowed to any player, and when one of the Batsmen is out the use of the bat shall not be allowed to any player until the next Batsman shall come in.

Notes

1 The umpires shall not award a match under this Law unless (i) 'Play' has been called in such a manner that both sides can clearly understand that play is to start, (ii) an appeal has been made, and (iii) they are satisfied that a side will not, or cannot, continue play.

2 It is an essential duty of the captains to ensure that the 'in-going' batsman passes the 'out-coming' one before the latter leaves the field of play. This is all the more important in view of the responsibility resting on the umpires for deciding whether or not the delay of the individual amounts to a refusal of the batting side to continue play.

3 The interval for luncheon should not exceed 45 minutes unless otherwise agreed (but *see* Law 10, Note 2). In the event of the last wicket falling within 2 minutes of the time arranged for luncheon or tea, the game shall be resumed at the usual hour, no allowance being made for the 10 minutes between the innings.

4 Bowling practice *on the pitch* is forbidden at any time during the game.

5 No bowler shall have a trial 'Run-up' after 'Play' has been called in any session, except at the fall of a wicket, when an umpire may allow such a trial 'Run-up', if he is satisfied that it will not cause any waste of time.

18 The Umpires shall call 'Time', and at the same time remove the bails from both wickets, on the cessation of play before any arranged interval, at the end of each day's play, and at the conclusion of the match. An 'Over' shall always be started if 'Time' has not been reached, and shall be completed unless a batsman is 'Out' or 'Retires' within 2 minutes of the completion of any period of play, but the 'Over' in progress at the close of play on the final day of a match shall be completed at the request of either Captain even if a wicket fall after 'Time' has been reached.

Notes

1 If, during the completion of the last over of any period of play, the players have occasion to leave the field, the Umpires shall call 'time.' In the case of the last over of the match, there shall be no resumption of play and the match shall be at an end.

2 The last over before an interval or the close of play shall be started, provided the umpire standing at square leg, after walking at his normal pace, has arrived at his position behind the stumps at the bowler's end before time has been reached. The above provision will apply if the batsman is 'Out' off, or 'Retires' after the last ball of an over when less than two minutes remain for play at the conclusion of the match.

3 In the final stages of a match, the umpires shall indicate when one hour of playing time remains (according to the agreed hours of play). From that moment, and providing a result is not reached earlier, the game will continue for a minimum of 20 6-ball overs (15 8-ball overs).

In the event of play being interrupted (including intervals or stoppages for rain, bad light, etc.), the number of overs to be bowled shall be reduced in proportion to the time lost, in the ratio of one over for every three minutes (four minutes for 8-ball overs) or part thereof lost.

If a new innings starts within the last hour of a match, the minimum number of overs to be bowled shall be calculated on the basis of one for each three minutes, or part of three minutes (four minutes for 8-ball overs) remaining for play, when the innings is started.

Whenever the minimum number of overs has been bowled before the agreed time for the close of play, the match shall continue (in the absence of a result) until the agreed time for close of play.

(Both captains may agree before the match to forgo the conditions of this Note subject to such agreement being permitted by 'Special Regulations'.)

Scoring

19 The score shall be reckoned by runs. A run is scored:—

1st So often as the Batsmen after a hit, or at any time while the ball is in play, shall have crossed and made good their ground from end to end; but if either Batsman run a short run, the Umpire shall call and signal 'One short' and that run shall not be scored. The Striker being caught, no run shall be scored; a Batsman being run out, that run which was being attempted shall not be scored.

2nd For penalties under Laws 21, 27, 29, 44 and boundary allowances under Law 20.

Notes

1 If while the ball is in play, the batsmen have crossed in running, neither returns to the wicket he has left except in the case of a boundary hit, or a boundary from extras, or under Laws 30 Note 1 and 46 Note 4 (vii). This rule applies even should a short run have been called, or should no run be reckoned as in the case of a catch.

2 A run is 'short' if either or both, batsmen fail to make good their ground in turning for a further run.

Although such a 'short' run shortens the succeeding one, the latter, if completed, counts. Similarly a batsman taking stance in front of his popping crease may run from that point without penalty.

3 (i) One run only is deducted if both batsmen are short in one and the same run.

(ii) Only if three or more runs are attempted can more than one run be 'short' and then, subject to (i) above, all runs so called shall be disallowed.

(iii) If either or both batsmen deliberately run short, the umpire is justified in calling 'Dead Ball' and disallowing any runs attempted or scored as soon as he sees that the fielding side have no chance of dismissing either batsman under the Laws.

4 An umpire signals 'short' runs when the ball becomes 'dead' by bending his arm upwards to touch the shoulder with the tips of his fingers. If there has been more than one 'short' run the umpires must instruct the scorers as to the number of runs disallowed. (*See* Note 1 to Law 4).

Boundaries

20 Before the toss for innings the Umpires shall agree with both sides on the Boundaries for play, and on the allowances to be made for them. An Umpire shall call or signal 'Boundary' whenever, in his opinion, a ball in play hits, crosses or is carried over the Boundary. The runs completed at the instant the ball reaches the Boundary shall count only should they exceed the allowance, but if the 'Boundary' result from an overthrow or from the wilful act of a fieldsman, any runs already made and the allowance shall be added to the score.

Notes

1 If flags or posts are used to mark a boundary, the real or imaginary line joining such points shall be regarded as the boundary, which should be marked by a white line if possible.

2 In deciding on the allowances to be made for boundaries the umpires will be guided by the prevailing custom of the ground.

3 It is a 'Boundary' if the ball touches any boundary line or if a fieldsman with ball in hand grounds any part of his person on or over that line. A fieldsman, however, standing within the playing area may lean against or touch a boundary fence in fielding a ball (*See also* Law 35, Note 5).

4 An obstacle, or person, within the playing area is not regarded as a boundary unless so arranged by the umpires. The umpire is not a boundary, but sight screens within the playing area shall be so regarded.

5 The customary allowance for a boundary is 4 runs, but it is usual to allow 6 runs for all hits pitching over and clear of the boundary line or fence (even though the ball has been previously touched by a fieldsman). It is not usual to allow 6 runs when a ball hits a sight screen full pitch, if the latter is on or inside the boundary.

6 In the case of a boundary resulting from either an overthrow or the wilful act of a fieldsman, the run in progress counts provided that the batsmen have crossed at the instant of the throw or act.

7 The umpire signals 'Boundary' by waving an arm from side to side, or a boundary '6' by raising both arms above the head.

Lost Ball

21 If a ball in play cannot be found or recovered any Fieldsman may call 'Lost Ball', when 6 runs shall be added to the score; but if more than 6 have been run before 'Lost Ball' be called, as many runs as have been run shall be scored.

The Result

22 A match is won by the side which shall have scored a total of runs in excess of that scored by the opposing side in its two completed innings; one-day matches, unless thus played out, shall be decided by the first innings. A match may also be determined by being given up as lost by one of the sides, or in the case governed by Law 17. A match not determined in any of these ways shall count as a 'Draw.'

Notes

1 It is the responsibility of the captains to satisfy themselves on the correctness of the scores on the conclusion of play.

2 Neither side can be compelled to continue after a match is finished; a one-day match shall not be regarded as finished on the result of the first innings if the umpires consider there is a prospect of carrying the game to a further issue in the time remaining.

3 The result of a finished match is stated as a win by runs, except in the case of a win by the side batting last, when it is by the number of wickets still then to fall. In a one-day match which is not played out on the second innings, this rule applies to the position at the time when a result on the first innings was reached.

4 A 'Draw' is regarded as a 'Tie' when the scores are equal at the conclusion of play but only if the match has been played out. If the scores of the completed first innings of a one-day match are equal, it is a 'Tie', but only if the match has not been played out to a further conclusion.

The Over

23 The ball shall be bowled from each wicket alternately in Overs of either 8 or 6 balls according to the agreed conditions of play. When the agreed number have been bowled and it has become clear to the Umpire at the Bowler's wicket that both sides have ceased to regard the ball as in play, the Umpire shall call 'Over' in a distinct manner before leaving the wicket. Neither a 'No Ball' nor a 'Wide Ball' shall be reckoned as one of the 'Over.'

Note

1 In the United Kingdom the 'over' shall be 6 balls, unless an agreement to the contrary has been made.

24 A bowler shall finish an 'Over' in progress unless he be incapacitated or be suspended for unfair play. He shall be allowed to change ends as often as desired, provided only that he shall not bowl two 'Overs' consecutively in one innings. A Bowler may require the Batsman at the wicket from which he is bowling to stand on whichever side of it he may direct.

Dead Ball

25 The ball shall be held to be 'Dead'—on being in the opinion of the Umpire finally settled in the hands of the Wicket-keeper or of the Bowler; or on reaching or pitching over the boundary; or, whether played or not, on lodging in the dress of either a Batsman or Umpire; or on the call of 'Over' or 'Time' by the Umpire; or on a Batsman being out from any cause: or on any penalty being awarded under Laws 21 or 44. The Umpire shall call 'Dead Ball' should he decide to intervene under Law 46 in a case of unfair play or in the event of a serious injury to a player; or should he require to suspend play prior to the Striker receiving a delivery. The ball shall cease to be 'Dead' on the Bowler starting his run or bowling action.

Notes

1 Whether the ball is 'finally settled' is a question of fact for the umpire alone to decide.

2 An umpire is justified in suspending play prior to the striker receiving a delivery in any of the following circumstances:—

  (i) If satisfied that, for an *adequate* reason, the striker is not ready to receive the ball, and makes no attempt to play it.
  (ii) If the bowler drops the ball accidentally before delivery, or if the ball does not leave his hand for any reason.
  (iii) If one or both bails fall from the striker's wicket before he receives the delivery.

In such cases the ball is regarded as 'Dead' from the time it last came into play.

3 A ball does not become 'Dead' when it strikes an umpire (unless it lodges in his dress), when the wicket is broken or struck down (unless a batsman is out thereby), or when an unsuccessful appeal is made.

4 For the purpose of this and other Laws, the term 'dress' includes the equipment and clothing of players and umpires as normally worn.

No Ball

26 For a delivery to be fair the ball must be bowled, not thrown or jerked; if either Umpire be not entirely satisfied of the absolute fairness of a delivery in this respect, he shall call and signal 'No Ball' instantly upon delivery. The Umpire at the Bowler's wicket shall call and signal 'No Ball' if he is not satisfied that at the instant of delivery the Bowler has at least some part of one foot behind

the Bowling crease and within the Return crease, and not touching or grounded over either crease.

Notes

1 Subject to the provisions of the Law being complied with a bowler is not debarred from delivering the ball with both feet behind the bowling crease.

2 The striker is entitled to know whether the bowler intends to bowl over or round the wicket, overarm or underarm, right or left handed. An umpire may regard any failure to notify a change in the mode of delivery as 'unfair', if so, he should call 'No ball.'

3 It is a 'No Ball' if the bowler before delivering a ball throws it at the striker's wicket even in an attempt to run him out (*See* Law 46, Note 4 (vii)).

4 If a bowler break the near wicket with any part of his person, during the delivery, such act in itself does not constitute 'No Ball.'

5 The umpire signals 'No Ball' by extending one arm horizontally.

6 An umpire should revoke the call 'No Ball' if the ball does not leave the bowler's hand for any reason.

27 The ball does not become 'Dead' on the call of 'No Ball.' The Striker may hit a 'No Ball' and whatever runs result shall be added to his score, but runs made otherwise from a 'No Ball' shall be scored 'No Balls,' and if no runs be made one run shall be so scored. The Striker shall be out from a 'No Ball' if he break Law 37, and either Batsman may be run out, or given out if he break Laws 36 or 40.

Notes

1 The penalty for a 'No Ball' is only scored if no runs result otherwise.

2 Law 46 Note 4 (vii) covers attempts to run before the ball is delivered, but should the non-striker unfairly leave his ground too soon, the fielding side may run out the batsman at the bowler's end by any recognised method. If the bowler throws at the near wicket, the umpire does not call 'No Ball,' though any runs resulting are so scored. The throw does not count in the 'Over.'

Wide Ball

28 If the Bowler shall bowl the ball so high over or so wide of the wicket that in the opinion of the Umpire it passes out of reach of the Striker, and would not have been within his reach when taking guard in the normal position, the Umpire shall call and signal 'Wide Ball' as soon as it shall have passed the Striker.

Notes

1 If a ball which the umpire considers to have been delivered comes to rest in front of the striker 'Wide' should not be called, and no runs should be added to the score unless they result from the striker hitting the ball which he has a right to do without interference by the fielding side. Should the fielding side interfere, the umpire is justified in replacing the ball where it came to rest and ordering the fieldsmen to resume the places they occupied in the field before the ball was delivered.

2 The umpire signals 'Wide' by extending both arms horizontally.

3 An umpire should revoke the call if the striker hits a ball which has been called 'Wide.'

29 The ball does not become 'Dead' on the call of 'Wide Ball.' All runs that are run from a 'Wide Ball' shall be scored 'Wide Balls,' or if no runs be made one run shall be so scored. The Striker may be out from a 'Wide Ball' if he breaks Laws 38 or 42, and either Batsman may be run out, or given out if he break Laws 36 or 40.

Bye and Leg Bye

30 If the ball, not having been called 'Wide' or 'No Ball,' pass the Striker without touching his bat or person, and any runs be obtained, the Umpire shall call or signal 'Bye'; but if the ball touch any part of the Striker's dress or person except his hand holding the bat, and any run be obtained, the Umpire shall call or signal 'Leg Bye'; such runs to be scored 'Byes' and 'Leg Byes' respectively.

Notes

1 The umpire shall regard the deliberate deflection of the ball by any part of the striker's person, except the hand holding the bat, as unfair, and as soon as he is satisfied that the fielding side have no chance of dismissing either batsmen as an immediate result of such action, he shall, without delay, call 'dead ball.' In deciding whether such deflection is deliberate, the criterion shall be whether or not the batsman has attempted to play the ball with his bat.

2 The umpire signals 'Bye', by raising an open hand above the head, and 'Leg Bye' by touching a raised knee with the hand.

The Wicket is Down

31 The wicket shall be held to be 'Down' if either the ball or the Striker's bat or person completely removes either bail from the top of the stumps or, if both bails be off, strikes a stump out of the ground. Any player may use his hand or arm to put the wicket down or, even should the bails be previously off, may pull up a stump, provided always that the ball is held in the hand or hands so used.

Notes

1 A wicket is not 'down' merely on account of the disturbance of a bail, but it is 'down' if a bail in falling from the wicket lodges between two of the stumps.

2 If one bail is off, it is sufficient for the purpose of this Law to dislodge the remaining one in any

of the ways stated, or to strike any of the three stumps out of the ground.

3 If, owing to the strength of the wind, the captains have agreed to dispense with the use of bails (see Law 8, Note 2), the decision as to when the wicket is 'down' is one for the umpires to decide on the facts before them. In such circumstances the wicket would be held to be 'down' even though a stump has not been struck out of the ground.

4 If the wicket is broken while the ball is in play, it is not the umpire's duty to remake the wicket until the ball has become 'dead'. A fieldsman, however, may remake the wicket in such circumstances.

5 For the purpose of this and other Laws the term 'person' includes a player's dress as defined in Law 25, Note 4.

Out of His Ground

32 A Batsman shall be held to be 'Out of his ground' unless some part of his bat in hand or of his person be grounded behind the line of the Popping Crease.

Batsman Retiring

33 A Batsman may retire at any time, but may not resume his innings without the consent of the opposing Captain, and then only on the fall of a wicket.

Note

1 When a batsman has retired owing to illness, injury, or some other unavoidable cause, his innings is recorded as 'Retired, Not out,' but otherwise as a completed innings to be recorded as 'Retired, Out.'

Bowled

34 The Striker is out 'Bowled'—If the wicket be bowled down, even if the ball first touch his bat or person.

Notes

1 The striker, after playing the ball, is out 'Bowled' if he then kicks or hits it on to his wicket before the completion of his stroke.

2 The striker is out 'Bowled' under this Law when the ball is deflected on to his wicket off his person, even though a decision against him might be justified under Law 39 L.B.W.

Caught

35 The Striker is out 'Caught'—If the ball, from a stroke of the bat or of the hand holding the bat, but not the wrist, be held by a Fieldsman before it touch the ground, although it be hugged to the body of the catcher, or be accidentally lodged in his dress. The Fieldsman must have both his feet entirely within the playing area at the instant the catch is completed.

Notes

1 Provided the ball does not touch the ground, the hand holding it may do so in effecting a catch.

2 The umpire is justified in disregarding the fact that the ball has touched the ground, or has been carried over the boundary provided that a catch has in fact been completed prior to such occurrence.

3 The fact that a ball has touched the striker's person before or after touching his bat does not invalidate a catch.

4 The striker may be 'Caught' even if the fieldsman has not touched the ball with his hands, including the case of a ball lodging in the wicket-keeper's pads.

5 A fieldsman standing within the playing area may lean against a boundary to catch a ball, and this may be done even if the ball has passed over the boundary.

6 If the striker lawfully plays the ball a second time he may be out under this Law, but only if the ball has not touched the ground since being first struck.

7 The striker may be caught off any obstruction within the playing area provided it has not previously been decided on as a boundary.

Handled the Ball

36 Either Batsman is out 'Handled the Ball'—If he touch it while in play with his hands, unless it be done at the request of the opposite side.

Notes

1 A hand holding the bat is regarded as part of it for the purposes of Laws 36, 37, and 39.

2 The correct entry in the score book when a batsman is given out but under this Law is 'Handled the Ball,' and the bowler does not get credit for the wicket.

Hit the Ball Twice

37 The Striker is out 'Hit the ball twice'—If the ball be struck or be stopped by any part of his person, and he wilfully strike it again, except for the sole purpose of guarding his wicket, which he may do with his bat or any part of his person, other than his hands. No runs except those which result from an overthrow shall be scored from a ball lawfully struck twice.

Notes

1 It is for the umpire to decide whether the ball has been so struck a second time legitimately or not. The umpire may regard the fact that a run is attempted as evidence of the batsmen's intention to take advantage of the second stroke, but it is not conclusive.

2 A batsman may not attempt to hit the ball twice, if in so doing he baulks the wicket-keeper or any fieldsman attempting to make a catch.

3 This Law is infringed if the striker, after playing the ball and without any request from the

opposite side, uses his bat to return the ball to a fieldsman.

4 The correct entry in the score book when the striker is given out under this Law is 'Hit the ball twice,' and the bowler does not get credit for the wicket.

Hit Wicket

38 The Striker is out 'Hit wicket'—If in playing at the ball he hit down his wicket with his bat or any part of his person.

Notes

1 The striker is 'Out' under this Law if:—

(i) In making a second stroke to keep the ball out of his wicket he hits it down.

(ii) While playing at the ball, but not otherwise, his wicket is broken by his cap or hat falling, or by part of his bat.

2 A batsman is not out for breaking the wicket with his bat or person while in the act of running.

L.B.W.

39 The Striker is out 'Leg before wicket'—If with any part of his person except his hand, which is in a straight line between wicket and wicket, even though the point of impact be above the level of the bails, he intercept a ball which has not first touched his bat or hand, and which, in the opinion of the Umpire, shall have, or would have, pitched on a straight line from the Bowler's wicket to the Striker's wicket, or shall have pitched on the off-side of the Striker's wicket, provided always that the ball would have hit the wicket.

Notes

1 The word 'hand' used in this Law should be interpreted as the hand holding the bat.

2 A batsman is only 'Out' under this Law if *all* the four following questions are answered in the affirmative.

(i) Would the ball have hit the wicket?

(ii) Did the ball pitch on a straight line between wicket and wicket (and this case includes a ball intercepted full pitch by the striker), or did it pitch on the off-side of the striker's wicket?

(iii) Was it part of the striker's person other than the hand which first intercepted the ball?

(iv) Was that part of the striker's person in a straight line between wicket and wicket at the moment of impact, irrespective of the height of the point of impact?

Obstructing the Field

40 Either Batsman is out 'Obstructing the field'—If he wilfully obstruct the opposite side; should such wilful obstruction by either Batsman prevent a ball from being caught it is the Striker who is out.

Notes

1 The umpire must decide whether the obstruction was 'wilful' or not. The involuntary interception by a batsman while running of a throw in is not in itself an offence.

2 The correct entry in the score book when a batsman is given out under this Law is 'Obstructing the field,' and the bowler does not get credit for the wicket.

Run Out

41 Either Batsman is out 'Run out'—If in running or at any time, while the ball is in play, he be out of his ground, and his wicket be put down by the opposite side. If the batsmen have crossed each other, he that runs for the wicket which is put down is out; if they have not crossed, he that has left the wicket which is put down is out. But unless he attempt to run, the Striker shall not be given 'Run out' in the circumstances stated in Law 42, even should 'No Ball' have been called.

Note

1 If the ball is played on to the opposite wicket, neither batsman is liable to be 'Run out' unless the ball has been touched by a fieldsman before the wicket is put down.

Stumped

42 A Striker is out 'Stumped'—If in receiving a ball, not being a 'No Ball,' delivered by the Bowler, he be out of his ground otherwise than in attempting a run, and the wicket be put down by the Wicket-keeper without the intervention of another fieldsman. Only when the ball has touched the bat or person of the Striker may the Wicket-keeper take it in front of the wicket for this purpose.

Note

1 The striker may be 'Stumped' if the wicket is broken by a ball rebounding from the wicket-keeper's person.

The Wicket-Keeper

43 The Wicket-keeper shall remain wholly behind the wicket until a ball delivered by the Bowler touches the bat or person of the Striker, or passes the wicket, on until the Striker attempts a run. Should the Wicket-keeper contravene this Law, the Striker shall not be out except under Laws 36, 37, 40, and 41 and then only subject to Law 46.

Notes

1 This Law is provided to secure to the striker his right to play the ball and to guard his wicket without interference from the wicket-keeper. The striker may not be penalised if in the legitimate defence of his wicket he interferes with the wicket-keeper, except as provided for in Law 37, Note 2.

2 If, in the opinion of the umpire, the encroachment by the wicket-keeper has not gained any advantage for the fielding side, nor in any way has interfered with the right of the striker to play the ball with complete freedom, nor has had any

effect whatsoever on the dismissal of the striker, he shall disregard the infringement.

The Fieldsman

44 The Fieldsman may stop the ball with any part of his person, but if he wilfully stop it otherwise five runs shall be added to the run or runs already made; if no run has been made five shall be scored. The penalty shall be added to the score of the Striker if the ball has been struck, but otherwise to the score of Byes, Leg Byes, No Balls or Wides as the case may be.

Notes

1 A fieldsman must not use his cap, etc., for the purpose of fielding a ball.

2 The five runs are a penalty and the batsmen do not change ends.

3 The number of on-side fielders behind the popping crease at the instant of the bowler's delivery shall not exceed two. In the event of infringement by the fielding side, the square-leg Umpire shall call 'No Ball'.
Note: The Umpire may elect to stand on the off-side, provided he informs the Captain of the fielding side and the Striker of his intention to do so.

(E) Duties of the Umpires

45 Before the toss for innings, the Umpires shall acquaint themselves with any 'Special Regulations', and shall agree with both Captains on any other conditions affecting the conduct of the match; shall satisfy themselves that the wickets are properly pitched; and shall agree, between themselves on the watch or clock to be followed during play.

Notes

1 Apart from 'Special Regulations' other conditions of play within the framework of the Laws are frequently necessary, *e.g.* Hours of play, Intervals, etc.

2 The captains are entitled to know which clock or watch will be followed during play.

46 Before and during a match the Umpires shall ensure that the conduct of the game and the implements used are strictly in accordance with the Laws; they are the sole judges of fair and unfair play, and the final judges of the fitness of the ground, the weather and the light for play in the event of the decision being left to them; all disputes shall be determined by them, and if they disagree the actual state of things shall continue. The Umpires shall change ends after each side has had one innings.

Notes

1 An umpire should stand where he can best see any act upon which his decision may be required. Subject to this over-riding consideration the umpire at the bowler's end should stand where he does not interfere with either the bowler's run up or the striker's view. The other umpire may elect to stand on the off instead of the leg side of the pitch, provided he informs the captain of the fielding side and the striker of his intention to do so.

2 The umpires must not allow the attitude of the players or spectators to influence their decisions under the Laws.

3 A code of signals for umpires is laid down in Notes to the relevant Laws; but an umpire must call as well as signal, if necessary, to inform the players and scorers.

4 FAIR AND UNFAIR PLAY.

(i) The umpires are entitled to intervene without appeal in the case of unfair play, but should not otherwise interfere with the progress of the game, except as required to do so by the Laws.

(ii) In the event of a player failing to comply with the instructions of an umpire or criticising his decisions, the umpires should in the first place request the captains to take action, and if this proves ineffective, report the incident forthwith to the executives of the teams taking part in the match.

(iii) It is illegal for a player to lift the seam of the ball in order to obtain a better hold. In such a case the umpire will if necessary change the ball for one which has had similar wear, and will warn the captain that the practice is unfair. The use of resin, wax, etc., by bowlers is also unfair, but a bowler may dry the ball when wet on a towel or with sawdust.

(iv) An umpire is justified in intervening under this Law should any player of the fielding side incommode the striker by any noise or motion while he is receiving a ball.

(v) It is the duty of umpires to intervene and prevent players from causing damage to the pitch which may assist the bowlers.

(vi) The persistent bowling of fast short-pitched balls at the batsman is unfair if, in the opinion of the umpire at the bowler's end, it constitutes a systematic attempt at intimidation. In such event he must adopt the following procedure:—

(a) When he decides that such bowling is becoming persistent he forthwith 'cautions' the bowler.

(b) If this 'caution' is ineffective, he informs the captain of the fielding side and the other umpire of what has occurred.

(c) Should the above prove ineffective, the umpire at the bowler's end must:—

(i) At the first repetition call 'Dead Ball,' when the over is regarded as completed.

    (ii) Direct the captain of the fielding side to take the bowler off forthwith. The captain shall take the bowler off as directed.

    (iii) Report the occurrence to the captain of the batting side as soon as an interval of play takes place.

    A bowler who has been 'taken off' as above may not bowl again during the same innings.

(vii) Any attempt by the batsmen to *steal a run* during the bowler's run up is unfair. Unless the bowler throws the ball at either wicket (*see* Laws 26, Note 3, and 27, Note 2), the umpire should call 'Dead Ball' as soon as the batsmen cross in any such attempt to run, after which they return to their original wickets.

(viii) No player shall leave the field for the purpose of having a rub down or shower while play is actually in progress.

5 GROUND, WEATHER AND LIGHT.

  (i) Unless agreement to the contrary is made before the start of a match, the captains (during actual play the batsmen at the wickets may deputise for their captain) may elect to decide in regard to the fitness of the ground, weather or light for play; otherwise or in the event of disagreement, the umpires are required to decide.

  (ii) Play should only be suspended when the conditions are so bad that it is unreasonable or dangerous for it to continue. The ground is unfit for play when water stands on the surface or when it is so wet or slippery as to deprive the batsmen or bowlers of a reasonable foothold, or the fieldsmen of the power of free movement. Play should *not* be suspended merely because the grass is wet and the ball slippery.

  (iii) After any suspension of play, the captains, or, if the decision has been left to them, the umpires, unaccompanied by any of the players, will without further instructions carry out an inspection immediately the conditions improve, and will continue to inspect at intervals. Immediately the responsible parties decide that play is possible, they must call upon the players to resume the game.

Appeals

47 The Umpires shall not order a Batsman out unless appealed to by the other side which shall be done prior to the delivery of the next ball, and before 'Time' is called under Law 18. The Umpire at the Bowler's wicket shall answer appeals before the other Umpire in all cases except those arising out of Laws 38 or 42 and out of Law 41 for run out at the Striker's wicket. In any case in which an Umpire is unable to give a decision, he shall appeal to the other Umpire whose decision shall be final.

Notes

1 An appeal, 'How's that?' covers all ways of being out (within the jurisdiction of the umpire appealed to), unless a specific way of getting out is stated by the person asking. When either umpire has given a batsman 'Not out' the other umpire may answer any appeal within the jurisdiction, provided it is made in time.

2 The umpire signals 'Out' by raising the index finger above the head. If the batsman is not out, the umpire calls 'Not out.'

3 An umpire may alter his decision provided that such alteration is made promptly.

4 Nothing in this Law prevents an umpire before giving a decision from consulting the other umpire on a point of fact which the latter may have been in a better position to observe. An umpire should not appeal to the other umpire in cases on which he could give a decision, merely because he is unwilling to give that decision. If after consultation he is still in any doubt, the principle laid down in Law 46 applies and the decision will be in favour of the batsman.

5 The umpires should intervene if satisfied that a batsman, not having been given out, has left his wicket under a misapprehension.

6 Under Law 25 the ball is 'Dead' on 'Over' being called; this does not invalidate an appeal made prior to the first ball of the following 'Over,' provided the bails have not been removed by both umpires after 'Time' has been called.

Notes for Scorers and Umpires

1 (*a*) Law 4 explains the status of the scorers in relation to the umpires.

  (*b*) During the progress of the game, if two scorers have been appointed, they should frequently check the total to ensure that the score sheets agree.

  (*c*) The following method of entering 'No Balls' and 'Wides' (Laws 27 and 29) in the score sheet is recommended:—

    (i) If no run is scored from the bat off a 'No Ball,' the latter should be entered as an 'Extra,' and a dot placed in the bowling analysis with a circle round it to show that the ball does not count in the over.

    (ii) If runs are scored from the bat off a 'No Ball,' they should be credited to the striker, and entered in the bowling analysis with a circle round the figure. Such runs count against the bowler in his analysis even though the ball does not count in the over.

    (iii) All runs scored from 'Wide Balls' are entered as 'Extras,' and inserted in the bowler's analysis with a cross to indicate that the ball does not count in the over.

2 The following code of signalling between the umpires and the scorers has been approved:—

Boundaries—by waving the hand from side to side.

A boundary six—by raising both arms above the head.

Byes—by raising the open hand above the head.

Leg Byes—by touching a raised knee with the hand.

Wides—by extending both arms horizontally.

No Balls—by extending one arm horizontally.

The decision 'Out,'—by raising the index finger above the head.

'One Short'—by bending the arm upwards and by touching the top of the nearest shoulder with the tips of the fingers of one hand.

3 If the above instructions are properly carried out, cases of disagreement as regards the scores and the results of matches should not occur.

It is, however, important that the captains should satisfy themselves of the correctness of the scores on the conclusion of play, as errors cannot subsequently be corrected.

It should be noted that, in general, by accepting the result notified by the scorers, the captain of the losing side has thereby acquiesced in the 'playing out or giving up' of the match as stated in Law 22.

Regulations for Drying the Pitch and Ground in First-Class Matches

N.B.—*These regulations are primarily designed for First-class Cricket, and their application in whole or in part in other grades of Cricket is at the discretion of the ground, etc., authorities.*

1 Except as provided below, the existing regulations in regard to the rolling of the pitch and the fitness of the ground for play shall apply. (*See* Laws 10, 12 and 46).

2 (i) To enable play to proceed with the least possible delay after rain, the groundsman shall adopt every practical means to protect or rid the surface of the ground, *other than the pitch*, of water or dampness at any time except while play is in progress.

(ii) Prior to tossing for choice of innings the artificial drying of the pitch and outfield shall be at the discretion of the Groundsman. Thereafter and throughout the match the drying of the outfield may be undertaken at any time by the Groundsman, but the drying of the pitch shall be carried out only on the instructions and under the supervision of the Umpires. The Umpires shall be empowered to have the pitch dried without a reference to the Captains at any time they are of the opinion that it is unfit for play.

(iii) In wet weather, the Umpires shall see that the footholes made by the bowlers and batsmen are cleaned, dried and filled up with sawdust at any time during the match, although the game is not actually in progress.

The Groundsman, without instructions from the Umpires, may also clean out in this way foot-holes, provided they are not on any part of the pitch, more than 3ft 6ins (107.7 cm) in front of the Popping creases.

The drying of the footholds on the pitch itself may be undertaken, as directed by the Umpires, at any time. The Umpires may also direct the Groundsman to protect against further rain, marks made by the bowlers, even though they be more than 3ft 6in (107.7 cm) in front of the popping creases, provided they are not between wicket and wicket, with loose sawdust, which, however, shall be removed prior to the resumption of play.

(iv) The Umpires shall ascertain from the Groundsman before the commencement of a match, what equipment is available for drying the pitch artificially.

Any roller may be used, if the Umpires think desirable but only (except as laid down in paragraph (2) (v)) for the purpose of drying the pitch and making it fit for play, and not otherwise. This would allow Umpires to roll the pitch after drying it, say with a light roller, for a minute or two, should they consider it desirable.

(v) When the artificial drying of the pitch, under the supervision of the Umpires, coincides with any interval during the match, after the toss for choice of innings, the Umpires, and not the Captain of the batting side shall select the roller to be used.

(vi) The fact that the Umpires may have dried the pitch artificially does not take the decision as regards the fitness of the pitch and ground for play out of the hands of the Captains even though the Umpires may have selected the roller to be used for the drying process. Law 46, Note 5 (i) is applicable in such cases.

Facts and Figures

Australian batting averages

Name	State	Matches	Inns.	Highest Score	Not Out	Total Runs	Avge.
a'Beckett, E. L.	Victoria	3	5	41	—	133	26.60
Alexander, G.	Victoria	2	4	33	—	52	13.00
Alexander, H. H.	Victoria	1	2	17*	1	17	17.00
Alan, F. E.	Victoria	1	1	5	—	5	5.00
Allen, P. J.	Queensland	1	—	—	—	—	—
Allen,	N.S.W.	1	2	30	—	44	22.00
Andrews, T. J. E.	N.S.W.	13	19	94	—	541	28.47
Archer, K. A.	Queensland	3	5	48	—	152	30.40
Archer, R. G.	Queensland	12	20	49	1	294	15.47
Armstrong, W. W.	Victoria	42	71	158	9	2172	35.03
Badcock, C. L.	S.A.	7	12	118	1	160	14.54
Bannerman, A. C.	N.S.W.	28	50	94	2	1105	23.08
Bannerman, C.	N.S.W.	3	6	165*	1	239	47.80
Bardsley, W.	N.S.W.	30	49	193*	4	1487	33.04
Barnes, S. G.	N.S.W.	9	14	234	2	846	70.50
Barnett, B. A.	Victoria	4	8	57	1	195	27.85
Barrett, J. E.	Victoria	2	4	67	1	80	26.66
Benaud, R.	N.S.W.	27	41	97	2	767	19.66
Blackham, J. McC.	Victoria	35	62	74	11	800	15.63
Blackie, D. D. J.	Victoria	3	6	11*	3	24	8.06
Booth, B. C.	N.S.W.	15	26	112	5	824	39.23
Bonner, G. J.	Vic. & N.S.W.	17	30	128	—	512	17.00
Boyle, H. F.	Victoria	12	16	36*	4	153	12.75
Bradman, D. G.	N.S.W. & S.A.	37	63	334	7	5028	89.78
Bromley, E. H.	Victoria	2	4	26	—	38	9.50
Brown, W. A.	N.S.W. & Qld.	13	24	206*	1	980	42.60
Bruce, W.	Victoria	14	26	80	2	702	29.25
Burge, P. J.	Queensland	22	37	181	6	1179	38.03
Burke, J. W.	N.S.W.	14	28	101*	5	676	29.89
Burn, K. E.	Tasmania	2	4	19	—	41	10.25
Burton, F. J.	N.S.W.	2	4	2*	4	4	2.00
Callaway, S. T.	N.S.W.	3	6	41	1	87	17.40
Carkeek, W.	Victoria	3	2	5	1	5	5.00
Carter, H.	N.S.W.	21	35	72	4	776	25.03
Chappell, G. S.	S.A.	11	18	131	2	680	42.50
Chappell, I. M.	S.A.	19	34	118	2	1170	36.56
Charlton, P. C.	N.S.W.	2	4	11	—	29	7.25
Chipperfield, A. G.	N.S.W.	9	15	99	3	356	29.66
Colley, D. J.	N.S.W.	3	4	54	—	84	21.00
Collins, H. L.	N.S.W.	16	26	162	—	1012	38.93
Conningham, A.	Queensland	1	2	10	—	13	6.50
Connolly, A. N.	Victoria	8	12	14	6	19	3.16
Cooper, B. B.	Victoria	1	2	15	—	18	9.00
Cooper, W. H.	Victoria	2	3	7	1	13	6.50
Corling, G. E.	N.S.W.	5	4	3	1	5	1.66
Cottam, J.	N.S.W.	1	2	3	—	4	2.00
Cotter, A.	N.S.W.	16	29	45	1	377	13.46
Coulthard, G.	Victoria	1	1	6*	1	6	—
Cowper, R. M.	Victoria	9	15	307	1	686	49.00
Craig, I. D.	N.S.W.	2	4	38	—	55	13.75
Crawford, P.	N.S.W.	1	2	—	1	—	—
Darling, L. S.	Victoria	7	12	85	—	245	20.41
Darling, J.	S.A.	31	55	178	2	1632	30.79
Davidson, A. K.	N.S.W.	25	36	77*	5	750	24.19
de Courcy, J.	N.S.W.	3	6	41	1	81	16.20
Dell, A. R.	Queensland	1	2	3*	2	6	—
Donnan, H.	N.S.W.	5	10	15	1	75	8.33
Dooland, B.	S.A.	2	3	29	—	49	16.33
Duff, R. A.	N.S.W.	19	34	146	1	1079	32.69
Duncan, J. R. F.	Queensland	1	1	3	—	3	3.00
Eady, C. J.	Tasmania	2	4	10*	1	20	6.66
Eastwood, K. H.	Victoria	1	2	5	—	5	2.50
Ebeling, H. I.	Victoria	1	2	41	—	43	21.50
Edwards, J. D.	Victoria	3	6	26	1	48	9.60
Edwards, R.	W.A.	4	7	170*	1	291	48.50
Emery, S. H.	N.S.W.	2	Has not batted in any match.				
Evans, E.	N.S.W.	6	10	33	2	82	10.25
Fairfax, A. G.	N.S.W.	5	6	65	2	215	53.75
Favell, L.	S.A.	6	10	41	1	203	22.55
Ferris, J. J.	N.S.W.	8	16	20*	4	98	8.16
Fingleton, J. H.	N.S.W.	12	21	136	—	671	31.95
Fleetwood-Smith, L. O'B.	Victoria	7	9	16*	4	48	9.60
Francis, B. C.	N.S.W.	3	5	27	—	52	10.40
Freeman, E. W.	S.A.	2	3	21	—	37	12.33
Freer, F.	Victoria	1	1	28*	1	28	—
Garrett, T. W.	N.S.W.	19	33	51*	6	340	12.59
Gaunt, R. A.	Victoria	1	1	3	—	3	3.00
Gehrs, D. R. A.	S.A.	2	4	11	—	19	4.75
Giffen, G.	S.A.	31	53	161	—	1238	23.35
Giffen, W. F.	S.A.	3	6	3	—	11	1.83
Gleeson, J. W.	N.S.W.	14	19	30	2	131	7.70
Graham, H.	Victoria	6	10	107	—	301	30.10
Gregory, D. W.	N.S.W.	3	5	43	2	60	20.00
Gregory, E. J.	N.S.W.	1	2	11	—	11	5.50
Gregory, J. M.	N.S.W.	21	30	100	3	941	34.85
Gregory, R. G.	Victoria	2	3	80	—	153	51.00
Gregory, S. E.	N.S.W.	52	92	201	7	2193	25.80
Grimmett, C. V.	S.A.	22	34	50	6	366	13.07
Groube, T. U.	Victoria	1	2	11	—	11	5.50
Grout, A. T. W.	Queensland	22	26	74	4	301	13.68
Guest, C.	Victoria	1	1	11	—	11	11.00
Hammence, R. A.	S.A.	1	2	30*	1	31	31.00
Harry, J.	Victoria	1	2	6	—	8	4.00
Hartigan, R. J.	Queensland	2	4	116	—	170	42.50
Hartkopf, A. E. V.	Victoria	1	2	80	—	80	40.00
Harvey, M.	Victoria	1	2	31	—	43	21.50
Harvey, R. N.	Vic. & N.S.W.	37	68	167	5	2416	38.34
Hassett, A. L.	Victoria	24	42	137	1	1572	38.34
Hawke, N. J. N.	S.A.	12	13	37	5	115	14.37
Hazlitt, G. R.	Vic. & N.S.W.	6	9	34*	3	87	14.50
Hendry, H. L.	N.S.W. & Vic.	9	15	112	2	284	21.84
Hill, C.	S.A.	41	76	188	—	2660	35.46
Hill, J. C.	Victoria	2	4	8*	1	12	6.00
Hodges, J.	Victoria	2	4	8	1	10	3.33
Hole, G. B.	N.S.W. & S.A.	9	17	66	—	439	25.82
Hopkins, A. J.	N.S.W.	17	28	43	2	434	16.69
Horan, T.	Victoria	15	27	124	2	471	18.84
Hordern, H. V.	N.S.W.	5	10	49*	2	173	21.62
Hornibrook, P. M.	Queensland	6	7	26	1	60	10.00
Howell, W. P.	N.S.W.	16	24	35	6	143	7.94
Inverarity, R. J.	W.A.	5	9	56	1	160	20.00
Iredale, F. A.	N.S.W.	14	28	140	1	807	36.68
Ironmonger, H.	Victoria	6	12	8	3	18	2.00
Iverson, J.	Victoria	5	7	1*	3	3	0.75
Jackson, A. A.	N.S.W.	4	6	164	—	350	58.33
Jarvis, A. H.	S.A.	11	21	82	3	303	16.83
Jarman, B. N.	S.A.	7	11	41	3	111	13.87
Jenner, T. J.	S.A.	2	4	30	—	36	9.00
Jennings, C. B.	S.A. & Qld.	3	4	21	1	44	14.66
Johnson, I. W.	Victoria	22	35	77	6	485	16.72
Johnston, W. A.	Victoria	17	25	29	12	138	10.61
Jones, E.		18	25	20	1	130	5.41
Jones, S. P.	N.S.W.	12	24	87	4	428	21.40
Kelleway, C.	N.S.W.	18	30	147	2	874	31.21
Kelly, J. J.	N.S.W.	33	52	46*	17	613	17.51
Kelly, T. J. D.	Victoria	2	3	35	—	64	21.33
Kendall, T.	Victoria	2	4	17*	1	39	13.00
Kippax, A. F.	N.S.W.	13	20	100	1	753	34.22
Kline, L.	Victoria	2	2	4*	2	5	—

Name	State	Matches	Inns.	Highest Score	Not Out	Total Runs	Avge.
Langley, G. R.	S.A.	9	13	18	2	97	8.81
Laver, F.	Victoria	15	23	45	6	196	11.52
Lawry, W. M.	Victoria	30	51	166	4	2233	47.51
Lee, P. K.	S.A.	1	2	42	—	57	28.50
Lillee, D. K.	W.A.	7	10	10	4	26	4.33
Lindwall, R. R.	N.S.W. & Qld.	29	43	100	7	795	22.08
Love, H. S.	N.S.W.	1	2	5	—	8	4.00
Loxton, S. J.	Victoria	6	8	93	—	219	27.37
Lyons, J. J.	S.A.	14	27	134	—	731	27.07
Macartney, C. G.	N.S.W.	26	42	170	4	1640	43.15
Mackay, K. D.	Queensland	16	23	86*	1	497	22.59
Maddocks, L. V.	Victoria	5	9	69	—	156	17.33
Mailey, A. A.	N.S.W.	18	25	46*	8	201	11.82
Mallett, A. A.	S.A.	6	8	43*	1	115	16.42
Marr, A. P.	N.S.W.	1	2	5	—	5	2.50
Marsh, R. W.	W.A.	12	18	92*	2	457	30.46
Massie, H. H.	N.S.W.	9	16	55	—	249	15.56
Massie, R. A. L.	W.A.	4	5	18	—	22	4.40
Matthews, T. J.	Victoria	5	7	53	—	74	10.57
Mayne, E. R.	Victoria	1	Has not batted in any match.				
McAlister, P. A.	Victoria	8	16	41	1	252	16.80
McCabe, S. J.	N.S.W.	24	43	232	3	1931	48.27
McCool, C.	Queensland	5	7	104*	2	272	54.40
McCormick, E. L.	Victoria	7	9	17*	2	35	5.00
McDonald, C. C.	Victoria	15	28	170	1	1044	38.66
McDonald, E. A.	Victoria	8	9	36	4	101	20.20
McDonnell, P. S.	N.S.W. & Vic.	19	34	147	1	958	29.03
McKenzie, G. D.	W.A.	26	35	34	8	252	9.33
McKibbin, T. R.	N.S.W.	5	8	28*	2	88	14.66
McLaren, J. W.	Queensland	1	2	—	2	—	—
McLeod, C. E.	Victoria	17	29	112	5	573	23.87
McLeod, R. W.	Victoria	6	11	31	—	146	13.27
McShane, P. G.	Victoria	3	6	12*	1	26	5.20
Meckiff, I.	Victoria	4	5	5	—	9	2.25
Midwinter, W. E.	Victoria	8	14	37	1	174	13.30
McIlwraith, J.	Victoria	1	2	7	—	9	4.50
Miller, K. R.	Vic. & N.S.W.	29	49	145*	4	1511	33.57
Minnett, R. B.	N.S.W.	6	12	90	—	309	25.75
Misson, F. M.	N.S.W.	1	2	25*	1	25	25.00
Moroney, J.	N.S.W.	1	2	0	—	0	—
Morris, A. R.	N.S.W.	24	43	206	2	2080	50.73
Morris, S.	Victoria	1	2	10*	1	14	14.00
Moses, H.	N.S.W.	6	10	33	—	197	19.70
Moule, H.	Victoria	1	2	34	—	40	20.00
Murdoch, W. L.	N.S.W.	18	33	211	5	896	32.00
Musgrove, H.	Victoria	1	2	9	—	13	6.50
Nagel, L. E.	Victoria	1	2	21*	1	21	21.00
Nash, L. J.	Victoria	1	1	17	—	17	17.00
Noble, M. A.	N.S.W.	39	68	133	6	1905	30.72
Nothling, O. E.	Queensland	1	2	44	—	52	26.00
O'Brien, L. P. J.	Victoria	3	6	61	—	104	17.33
O'Connor, J. A.	S.A.	4	8	20	1	86	12.28
Oldfield, W. A.	N.S.W.	38	62	65	14	1116	23.25
O'Keeffe, K. J.	N.S.W.	2	3	27	—	42	14.00
O'Neill, N. C.	N.S.W.	19	30	117	3	1072	39.70
O'Reilly, W. J.	N.S.W.	19	32	42	6	277	10.65
Oxenham, R. K.	Queensland	3	5	39	—	88	17.60
Palmer, G. E.	Victoria	17	25	48	4	296	14.09
Park, R. L.	Victoria	1	1	—	—	—	—
Pellew, C. E.	S.A.	9	13	116	1	478	39.83
Philpott, P. I.	N.S.W.	3	4	10	1	22	7.33
Ponsford, W. H.	Victoria	20	35	266	2	1558	47.21
Pope, R.	N.S.W.	1	2	3	—	3	1.50
Ransford, V. S.	Victoria	15	29	143*	6	893	38.82
Redpath, I. R.	Victoria	18	31	171	3	1040	37.14
Reedman, J. C.	S.A.	1	2	17	—	21	10.50
Richardson, A. J.	S.A.	9	13	100	—	403	31.00
Richardson, V. Y.	S.A.	14	25	138	—	622	24.88
Rigg, K. E.	Victoria	3	5	47	—	118	23.60
Ring, D. T.	Victoria	2	3	18	—	34	11.33
Robertson, W. R.	Victoria	1	2	2	—	2	1.00
Robinson, R. H.	N.S.W.	1	2	3	—	5	2.50
Rorke, G.	N.S.W.	2	2	2*	2	2	—
Ryder, J.	Victoria	17	28	201*	4	1060	44.16
Saggers, R. A.	N.S.W.	1	1	5	—	5	5.00
Saunders, J. V.	Victoria	12	20	11*	5	34	2.26
Scott, H. J. H.	Victoria	8	14	102	1	359	27.61
Sheahan, A. P.	Victoria	9	16	124	3	341	26.23

Name	State	Matches	Inns.	Highest Score	Not Out	Total Runs	Avge.
Shepherd, B. K.	W.A.	2	3	71*	1	94	47.00
Sievers, M. W. S.	Victoria	3	6	25*	1	67	13.40
Simpson, R. B.	W.A. & N.S.W.	19	31	311	3	1405	50.17
Sincock, D. J.	S.A.	1	2	29	—	56	28.00
Slater, K.	W.A.	1	1	1*	1	1	—
Slight, J.	Victoria	1	2	11	—	11	5.50
Smith D.,	Victoria	2	3	24*	1	30	15.00
Spofforth, F. R.	N.S.W. & Vic.	18	29	50	6	217	9.43
Stackpole, K. R.	Victoria	14	24	207	1	1166	50.69
Taber, H. B.	N.S.W.	1	1	16	—	16	16.00
Tallon, D.	Queensland	15	20	92	2	340	18.88
Taylor, J. M.	N.S.W.	18	25	108	—	957	38.28
Thomas, G.	N.S.W.	3	4	52	—	147	36.75
Thompson, N.	N.S.W.	2	4	41	—	67	16.75
Thomson, A. L.	Victoria	4	5	12*	4	22	22.00
Toschack, E. R.	N.S.W.	9	9	20*	5	65	16.25
Travers, J. F.	S.A.	1	2	9	—	10	5.00
Tribe, G.	Victoria	3	3	25*	1	85	17.50
Trott, A. E.	Victoria	3	5	86*	3	206	103.00
Trott, G. H. S.	Victoria	24	42	143	—	921	21.92
Trumble, H.	Victoria	31	55	70	13	838	19.95
Trumble, J. W.	Victoria	7	13	59	1	243	20.25
Trumper, V. T.	N.S.W.	40	74	185*	5	2263	32.79
Turner, C. T. B.	N.S.W.	17	32	29	4	323	11.53
Veivers, T. R.	Queensland	9	10	67*	2	242	30.24
Waite, M. G.	S.A.	2	3	8	—	11	3.66
Wall, T. W.	S.A.	14	19	20	4	83	5.53
Walters, K. D.	N.S.W.	21	35	155	3	1180	36.87
Walters, F. H.	Vic. & N.S.W.	1	2	7	—	12	6.00
Ward, F. A.	S.A.	4	8	18	2	36	6.00
Watson, G. D.	W.A.	2	4	13	—	21	5.25
Watson, W.	N.S.W.	1	2	18	—	21	10.50
Whitty, W. J.	S.A.	6	8	14	4	35	8.75
Woodfull, W. M.	Victoria	25	41	155	3	1675	44.07
Woods, S. M. J.	N.S.W.	3	6	18	—	32	5.33
Worrall, J.	Victoria	11	22	76	3	478	25.15

*Signifies "Not Out".

Australian bowling averages

Name	Overs	Balls	Maidens	Runs	Wickets	Avge.
a'Beckett, E. L.	156	936	41	283	3	94.30
Alexander, G.	42	168	13	93	2	46.50
Alexander, H. H.	46	276	3	154	1	154.00
Allan, F. E.	45	180	15	80	4	20.00
Allan, P. J.	24	192	6	84	2	42.00
Andrews, T. J. E.	26	156	5	116	1	116.00
Archer, R. G.	374.5	2445	126	761	35	21.80
Armstrong, W. W.	1135.2	6812	360	2288	74	30.91
Bannerman, A. C.	73	292	17	163	4	40.75
Barnes, S. G.	50	314	5	118	1	118.00
Benaud, R.	1001	7132	289	2645	83	31.86
Blackie, D. D. J.	210	1260	51	444	14	31.71
Bonnor, G. J.	41	164	16	84	2	42.00
Booth, B. C.	.2	2	—	4	—	—
Boyle, H. F.	431	1724	173	641	32	20.03
Bradman, D. G.	16	96	3	51	1	51.00
Bromley, E. H.	10	60	4	19	—	—
Bruce, W.	211.1	954	71	440	12	36.66
Burke, J. W.	38	288	15	83	2	41.50
Callaway, S. T.	78.3	471	33	142	6	23.66
Chappell, G. S.	149.2	1080	35	380	7	54.28
Chappell, I. M.	96	672	25	264	4	66.00
Charlton, P. C.	9	45	7	24	3	8.00
Chipperfield, A. G.	131	872	27	409	5	81.80
Colley, D. J.	121.3	729	20	312	6	52.00
Collins, H. L.	74	522	16	236	3	78.66
Connolly, A. N.	332.1	2123	83	815	25	32.60
Coningham, A.	31	186	9	76	3	38.00
Cooper, W. H.	116.2	466	31	226	9	25.11
Corling, G. E.	193.1	1159	50	453	12	37.75
Cotter, A.	577.3	3465	63	1916	67	38.59
Cowper, R. M.	125	794	41	318	10	31.80
Crawford, P.	5	30	2	4	—	—

Name	Overs	Balls	Maidens	Runs	Wickets	Avge.
Darling, L. S.	27	162	7	65	—	—
Davidson, A. K.	856.3	5999	221	2003	84	23.84
Dell, A. R.	42.7	343	11	97	5	19.40
Dooland, B.	98	784	9	351	8	48.87
Donnan, H.	9	54	2	22	—	—
Duff, R. A.	30	180	8	85	4	21.25
Duncan, J. R. F.	14	112	4	30	—	—
Eady, C. J.	42.3	223	14	112	7	16.00
Eastwood, K. H.	5	40	—	21	1	21.00
Ebling, H. I.	31	186	9	90	3	30.00
Emery, S. H.	19	114	2	68	2	34.00
Evans, E.	316.2	1266	166	332	7	47.42
Fairfax, A. G.	168.2	1010	38	445	14	31.78
Ferris, J. J.	478.5	2030	224	684	48	14.25
Fleetwood-Smith, L.	349.3	2359	54	1192	33	36.12
Freeman, E. W.	67.5	407	17	194	6	32.33
Freer, F.	20	160	3	74	3	24.66
Garratt, T. W.	677	2708	297	970	36	26.90
Gaunt, R. A.	46	276	10	87	3	29.00
Giffen, G.	1277.1	6325	434	2791	103	27.09
Gleeson, J. W.	491.3	3391	150	1179	29	40.65
Gregory, D. W.	5	20	1	9	—	—
Gregory, J. M.	743	4872	110	2364	70	33.77
Gregory, R. G.	3	24	—	14	—	—
Gregory, S. E.	5	30	—	33	—	—
Grimmett, C. V.	1527.1	9227	427	3439	106	32.44
Guest, C.	18	144	—	59	—	—
Hartigan, R. J.	2	12	—	7	—	—
Hartkopf, A. E. V.	30	240	2	134	1	134.00
Harvey, R. N.	8	56	4	15	—	—
Hassett, A. L.	15	90	2	60	—	—
Hawke, N. J. N.	472	3176	128	1119	37	30.24
Hazlitt, G. R.	184.3	1107	49	443	16	27.68
Hendry, H. L.	232.1	1443	65	508	14	36.28
Hill, J. C.	66	396	18	159	7	22.71
Hodges, J.	46.2	186	9	84	6	14.00
Hole, G. B.	23	150	8	46	1	46.00
Hopkins, A. J.	197.1	1183	47	581	21	27.66
Horan, T.	93.1	373	45	143	11	13.00
Hordern, H. V.	277.2	1664	43	780	32	24.37
Hornibrook, P. M.	263.1	1579	63	667	17	39.23
Howell, W. P.	612	3508	229	1245	35	35.57
Inverarity, R. J.	62	372	26	93	4	23.25
Iredale, F. A.	2	12	—	3	—	—
Ironmonger, H.	407.4	2446	155	712	21	33.90
Iverson, J.	138.4	1108	29	320	21	15.23
Jenner, T. J.	65.6	526	15	176	6	29.33
Johnson, I. W.	651	4600	185	1590	42	37.85
Johnston, W. A.	778.5	5260	224	1855	75	24.78
Jones, E.	652.3	3586	146	1757	60	29.28
Jones, S. P.	65.2	262	26	112	6	18.66
Kelleway, C.	499.4	3340	112	1158	37	31.29
Kendall, T.	140.3	563	56	215	14	15.35
Kippax, A. F.	12	72	5	19	—	—
Kline, L.	25	200	6	77	—	—
Laver, F.	400.1	2369	122	961	37	25.97
Lawry, W. M.	1	8	1	4	—	—
Lee, P. K.	52.4	316	13	163	4	40.75
Lillee, D. K.	312.2	1993	88	747	39	19.15
Lindwall, R. R.	982.2	6729	216	2579	114	22.62
Loxton, S. J.	72	450	12	174	3	58.00
Lyons, J. J.	61.1	316	17	149	6	24.83
Macartney, C. G.	438.5	2633	120	908	33	27.51
Mackay, K. D.	427.6	2828	126	876	24	36.50
Mailey, A. A.	784.2	5197	91	2935	86	34.12
Mallett, A. A.	220.7	1439	55	621	21	29.57
Marr, A. P.	12	48	6	14	—	—
Massie, R. A. L.	199.1	1195	58	409	23	17.78
Matthews, T. J.	118.2	710	28	277	3	92.33
McCabe, S. J.	416.5	2585	84	1082	21	51.52
McCool, C.	182	1456	27	493	18	27.38
McCormick, E. L.	198	1356	26	696	21	33.14
McDonald, E. A.	331.5	1991	42	1060	33	33.12
McDonnell, P. S.	13	52	1	53	—	—
McKenzie, G. D.	1097.3	7483	233	3022	96	31.48
McKibbin, T. R.	183.2	1032	41	496	17	29.17
McLaren, J. W.	24	144	3	70	1	70.00
McLeod, C. E.	570.2	3374	172	1325	33	40.15
McLeod, R. W.	195.4	1089	67	384	12	32.00
McShane, P. G.	27	108	9	48	1	48.00
Meckiff, I.	112.2	898	24	303	17	17.82
Midwinter, W. E.	234.3	909	104	333	14	23.78
Miller, K. R.	757.1	5717	224	1960	87	22.56
Minnett, R. B.	69.1	415	15	231	9	23.66
Misson, F. M.	76	456	18	244	7	34.85
Morris, A. R.	11.5	71	1	39	1	39.00
Morris, S.	34	136	14	73	2	36.50
Moule, W. H.	12.3	51	4	23	3	7.66
Nagel, L. E.	43.4	262	9	110	2	55.00
Nash, L. J.	22.5	181	2	104	5	20.80
Noble, M. A.	1169.1	6845	353	2850	115	24.78
Nothling, O. E.	46	276	15	72	—	—
O'Connor, J. A.	115.2	692	24	340	13	26.15
O'Keeffe, K. J.	100	800	30	260	6	43.33
O'Neill, N. C.	49	364	10	176	2	88.00
O'Reilly, W. J.	1228	7846	439	2616	102	25.64
Oxenham, R. K.	201.1	1208	72	349	7	49.85
Palmer, G. E.	1129.3	4519	453	1678	78	21.51
Park, R. L.	1	6	—	9	—	—
Pellew, C. E.	13	78	3	34	—	—
Philpott, P. I.	100.1	801	9	373	8	46.62
Ransford, V. S.	3.1	19	1	19	—	—
Reedman, J. C.	9.3	57	2	24	1	24.00
Richardson, A. J.	264	1812	91	521	12	43.41
Ring, D. T.	71	426	20	174	3	58.00
Robertson, W. R.	11	44	3	24	—	—
Rorke, G.	70.5	565	17	172	8	21.50
Ryder, J.	241.5	1531	54	630	13	48.46
Saunders, J. V.	544.4	3268	108	1621	64	25.32
Scott, H. J. H.	7	28	1	26	—	—
Sievers, M. W. S.	75.2	602	25	164	9	18.22
Simpson, R. B.	266.4	1828	79	839	16	52.43
Sincock, D. J.	20	160	1	99	—	—
Slater, K.	32	256	9	101	2	50.50
Spofforth, F. R.	1046.1	4185	419	1731	94	18.41
Stackpole, K. R.	141.5	1099	32	410	4	102.50
Taylor, J. M.	8	48	1	26	1	26.00
Thompson, N.	28	12	16	31	1	31.00
Thomson, A. L.	190	1520	33	654	12	54.50
Toshack, E. R.	347.5	2435	120	811	28	28.96
Travers, J. F.	8	48	2	14	1	14.00
Tribe, G.	95	760	9	330	2	165.00
Trott, A. E.	79	474	17	192	9	21.33
Trott, G. H. S.	324.5	1887	47	1019	29	35.13
Trumble, H.	1396.3	7889	448	2945	141	20.88
Trumble, J. W.	150	600	59	222	10	22.20
Trumper, V. T.	58	348	17	140	2	70.00
Turner, C. T. B.	1052.4	5342	457	1670	101	16.53
Veivers, T. R.	295	1904	83	694	15	46.26
Waite, M. G.	92	552	23	191	1	191.00
Wall, T. W.	636.5	3821	115	1682	34	39.11
Walters, K. D.	161.5	1251	24	500	16	31.25
Ward, F. A.	166	1268	29	574	11	52.18
Watson, G. D.	40	240	14	92	3	30.66
Whitty, W. J.	217	1302	74	498	15	33.20
Woods, S. M. J.	54.1	217	18	121	5	24.20
Worrall, J.	63	255	29	127	1	127.00

Wides and no-balls counted as runs.

NOTE—The number of balls to the over in England was increased from four to five in May 1889, and from five to six in May 1900. In Australia the number was increased from four to six in December 1887, from six to eight in December, 1919, and reduced to six in 1928-29. In 1936-37 and subsequent seasons, eight balls were bowled to the over.

The averages were taken at the beginning of the 1973-74 season.